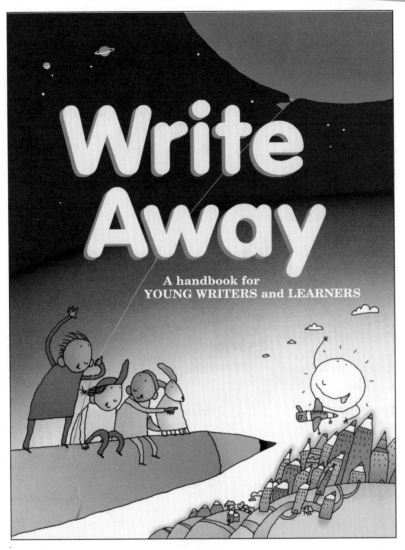

Write Away

A handbook for
YOUNG WRITERS and LEARNERS

Authors
Dave Kemper, Ruth Nathan, Patrick Sebranek

Illustrator Chris Krenzke

WRITE SOURCE®

GREAT SOURCE EDUCATION GROUP
a Houghton Mifflin Company

I(T)P® International Thomson Publishing
The ITP logo is a trademark under licence
www.thomson.com

Published in Canada in 1999 by

I(T)P® Nelson

A division of Thomson Canada Limited
1120 Birchmount Road
Scarborough, Ontario M1K 5G4
www.nelson.com

Acknowledgments

We're grateful to many people who helped bring *Write Away* to life. First, we must
thank all the students who contributed their writing models and ideas.

Also, thanks to the writers, editors, and teachers who helped make this book a reality.

Linda Bradley	Candyce Norvell
Laurie Cooper	Susan Ohanian
Connie Erdman	Laura Robb
Gale Hegeman	Charles Temple
Michelle Kerkman	Dawn Wenzel-Helnore
Dian Lynch	Sue Wind
Amy Nathan	

In addition, we want to thank our Write Source team for all their help: Laura Bachman,
Colleen Belmont, Carol Elsholz, Sherry Gordon, Lois Krenzke, Sue Paro, Julie Sebranek,
Sandy Wagner, and Dawn Weis.

Canadian Cataloguing in Publication Data

Kemper, Dave
    Write away: a handbook for young writers and learners

For use in grade 2 & 3.
Includes index.
ISBN 0-17-618661-1

1. English language — Composition and exercises — Juvenile literature.
I. Nathan, Ruth. II. Sebranek, Patrick. III. Title.

LB1576.K45 1999   808'.042   C98-932945-3

Printed and bound in Canada
    2 3 4 5 6 7 8 9 0 /TP/ 7 6 5 4 3 2 1 0 9

Up, Up, and Away!

The *Write Away* handbook is divided into five parts:

The Process of Writing This part helps you learn all about writing.

The Forms of Writing In here, you'll learn how to write letters, reports, stories, and more.

The Tools of Learning Reading, word study, and listening are important skills. This part covers them all.

The Proofreader's Guide When do you use periods and capital letters? You'll find out here.

The Student Almanac This part has animal facts, maps, math charts, and more!

4

Table of Contents

The PROCESS of Writing

The **FORMS** of Writing

6

The TOOLS of Learning

The Proofreader's GUIDE

The Student ALMANAC

BOOKS
to Grow In

There are books to grow in
and books to know in,

Books that really please you
and books that sometimes tease you,

Books you're glad you found
and books you can't put down,

Books with funny pictures
and books that make you richer,

Books with a friendly tone—
books you want, all for your own!

A Book Just for You

Write Away is a book "to grow in." It tells you all about writing and many other skills. *Write Away* will "please you" in many ways, too. It is full of fun pictures, charts, and models.

Doing Your Best Work

Think of *Write Away* as your special helper. It will help you do your best writing and learning. It is one book you will want, "all for your own!"

10

The
PROCESS
of Writing

12

All About Writing

Starting to Write

Why are these kids smiling? They know all about writing. And guess what? They want to share some of their ideas. Let's see what they have to say.

Read, Read, Read

Lindy wrote a story about a little girl and her grandmother. She got the idea after reading *Grandma's Secret* by Paulette Bourgeois. Here is her advice.

Pick Good Ideas

Roger just got his new cat, Henry. He wrote a letter to his aunt telling her all about Henry. Here is his writing tip:

Write about subjects that you really like. Then writing is fun.

Dear Aunt Jenny,
I just got my new cat. His name is Henry.

Try Different Forms

Jenna is always writing something. She writes poems, stories, and notes. She's even writing a riddle book! Here is her advice:

Try different forms of writing. Each one teaches you something new.

Practise, Practise, Practise

Octavio likes to write. He even writes at home, when he could be watching TV! Here is the most important thing he has learned:

To become a good writer, you have to practise. Try to write every day, like me!

Share Your Writing

Ben shares his writing with friends. He likes to see how much they like his stories. He always reads their stories, too. Here is his tip:

Share your stories and poems. Sharing helps everyone write better!

Have Fun

Maybe you are just learning to write. Or maybe you already write a lot. It doesn't really matter. You only need to follow Kayla's advice:

Using the Writing Process

There are five steps in the writing process. Follow these steps when you write.

1 PLAN

Think of subjects to write about.

Choose the best one.

List ideas about your subject.

2 WRITE

Write about your subject.

Don't worry about making mistakes.

3 REVISE

Read over your writing. **Change** parts to make it better.

4 CHECK

Check for . . .
* **Spelling**
* **Capital Letters**
* **Punctuation**

5 PUBLISH

Write a neat copy to share. (See pages 42-47 for more ideas.)

The Writing Process in Action

Casey had to write about her favourite animal. Let's follow along as she writes her story.

Casey thought about different animals. She decided to write about her dog, Muffy. Then she had to get ready to write. So she listed ideas about Muffy in a cluster.

2
WRITE

Next, Casey wrote about her ideas. She put the sentences in the best order. This is her first draft.

My Furry Friend

I like to play with my dog muffy. I sit on the skatebord and tie it. Then Muffy pulls me. When we play hide-and-seek she always finds me. When we race, she always wins. I realy like to watch her sleep and take naps. She falls sometimes when she rolls over.

REVISE

Then Casey tried to make her writing better. Here is one idea she added:

I like to play with my dog

muffy. I sit on the skatebord

and tie it. Then Muffy pulls me.
       her leash to

CHECK

Casey also checked her writing for spelling, capital letters, and punctuation. Here are two things she corrected:

capital letter   spelling

I like to play with my dog

M

muffy. I sit on the ~~skatebord~~
                skateboard

and tie it. Then Muffy pulls me.
       her leash to

PUBLISH

Casey wrote a neat copy of her story to share.

My Furry Friend

I like to play with my dog Muffy. I sit on the skateboard and tie her leash to it. Then Muffy pulls me. When we play hide-and-seek, she always finds me. When we race, she always wins. I really like to watch her take naps. When she rolls over, she sometimes falls off the sofa. It is so funny!

Later on, Casey may turn her story into a picture book!

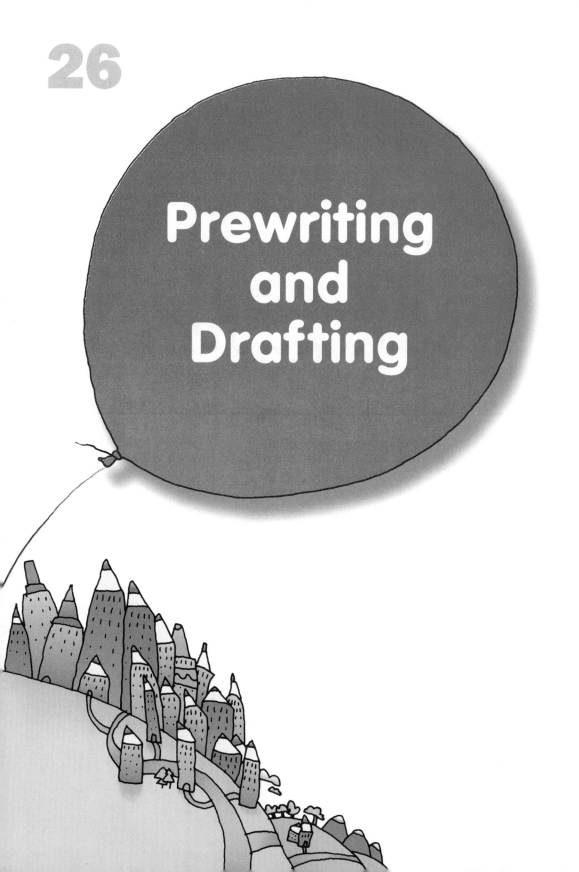

26

Prewriting and Drafting

Keeping an Idea Notebook

An **idea notebook** can be a treasure chest of writing ideas. Ideas for your notebook are all around you. You can write about recess and class trips, families and friends, special places and important happenings!

Notebook Models

Here are two example notebook pages.

Philip's Notebook

Brittany's Notebook

December 11

I learned to dive!
chin down
bend knees
arms out
fall in

shiver, shiver

December 1
   Our baby sitter
Anne is sick. I'm
sad!

Anne

Philip used his ideas in a
letter to his grandfather.
Brittany used her ideas in
a story.

Using Your Notebook

You can use your notebook ideas when you write. Here's how:

READ over your notebook often.

PICK a good idea to write about.

TELL a partner about it.

ASK if your partner has any questions or can tell you more about the subject.

WRITE everything down.

CHOOSE a way to write about your idea. Try a letter, a poem, a story, or another form.

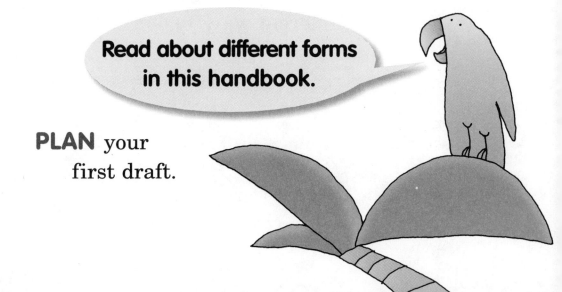

Read about different forms in this handbook.

PLAN your first draft.

Planning Your Writing

Planning helps you write your best stories and reports. Planning has three main parts:

1. Thinking of subjects to write about

2. Choosing the best one

3. Collecting ideas for writing

Collecting Ideas

It's important to collect ideas about your subject before you write. The next page names different ways to do this.

Gather, Talk, Think

There are three main ways to collect ideas.

GATHER facts from books, magazines, and CD's.

TALK to other people about your subject.

THINK about your subject by trying these things:

Listing ● Just list ideas about your subject on paper.

Clustering ● Write your subject in the middle of your paper and put ideas around it. (See page 232.)

Drawing ● Plan your writing by drawing pictures about your subject.

Writing the First Draft

You pick a subject and collect ideas about it. What's next? You put those ideas into sentences. That means you write your first draft.

Putting Things in Order

Try to put all of your sentences in the best order. But don't worry about making mistakes. You can make changes later on.

Drafting TIPS

PLAN your beginning. Here are three ways to begin.

Begin with a fact:
Dogs are usually furry.

Begin with a quotation:
"My dog is the strangest beast!"

Begin with a question:
Who would want a dog like mine?

WRITE the rest of your draft. Keep going until you get all of your ideas on paper.

SKIP every other line when you write. Then you will have space to make changes and add new words.

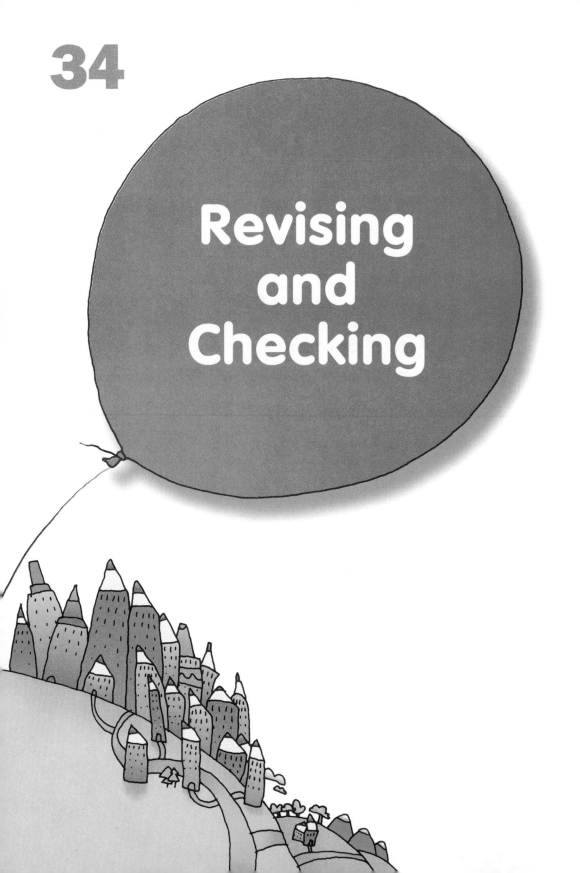

34

Revising and Checking

Revising Your Writing

Vilas goes to school in Winnipeg, Manitoba. He writes a lot of stories. Here is one important thing he has learned:

My writing will be good if I make changes to parts I don't like.

Making Changes

Making changes is an important part of the writing process. When you make changes, you are **revising**. You can learn about revising on the next two pages.

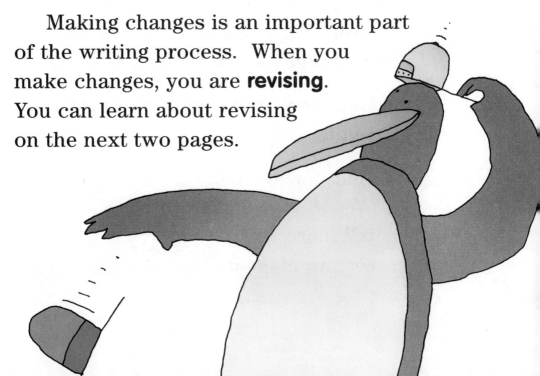

Revising TIPS

Follow these tips when you revise:

READ your first draft.

LOOK for parts that could be better.

HAVE your teacher or another person read your first draft, too.

FIND OUT what your reader likes. Find out what questions he or she has.

MAKE changes in your writing.

✔ Cross out parts that are not needed. (Some ideas may be off the subject.)

✔ Change words that don't sound right.

✔ Add new words. (You may need to tell more about certain ideas in your writing.)

Checking the Three Main Parts

Make sure your writing has a good beginning, middle, and ending.

Beginning

The beginning should name your subject in an interesting way.

> I surprised my aunt and my uncle when I went fishing with them.

Middle

The middle should tell about your subject.

> They always go to Eagle Lake. They think they are the best fishers on the lake. I caught three fish. My aunt and my uncle didn't catch any.

Ending

The ending should say something important about the subject.

> The next day they said I was the best fisher!

Writing Conferences

In a **writing conference**, your teacher or a partner helps you with your writing. Here are three good reasons to have a conference:

When Planning ● To help you pick a writing subject.

When Revising ● To help you improve a first draft.

When Checking ● To help you check your writing for errors.

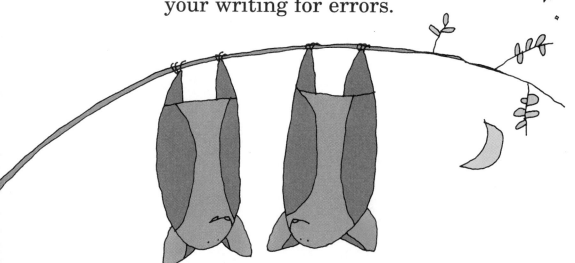

Working Together

Here's how revising conferences work:

What do your partners say?

1. They name the parts they really like in your writing.
2. Then they may ask questions about other parts:

   Can you tell me more about this idea?

   Does this part sound right to you?

What should you do?

1. Listen to what your partners say.
2. Answer any questions.
3. Try to make your first draft better.

Checking for Errors

When is your writing ready to publish? It is ready after you have checked it for errors and made a neat final copy. Checking for errors is called **proofreading**.

Work Carefully!

It's easy to miss errors. So you have to check your writing very carefully. Use the checklist and tips on the next page to help you proofread.

Proofreading TIPS

READ your writing aloud. Then you can listen for errors.

TOUCH each word with your pencil. This will help you check for spelling.

FIND a helper. Have your teacher or someone else check your writing, too.

Proofreading Checklist

✔ Did you capitalize the first word in each sentence?

✔ Did you capitalize names?

✔ Did you put a period, a question mark, or an exclamation point after each sentence?

✔ Did you spell your words correctly?

Publishing Your Writing

Publishing is sharing the final copy of your writing. To publish, you can read your stories to your classmates. You can also post your writing on a bulletin board.

Sharing Your Work

This chapter lists many other ways to publish. You will also learn about adding pictures and making books.

Publishing Ideas

MAKE a picture book for one of
your stories.

PUT TOGETHER a class book of stories
or poems.

ACT OUT your story or play.

PUT ON a puppet show.

DESIGN a birthday or holiday card
using your own poem.

PRINT a class newspaper.

READ your report to the
parent/teacher group.

SEND one of your best stories or
poems to a magazine. (Ask
your teacher for help.)

Adding Pictures

It can be fun to draw pictures to go with your writing. You can draw them before, while, or after you write.

Drawing One Picture

Sometimes one picture is all you need. Auburn wrote a poem about a bird called a quetzal (*say* ket sol′).

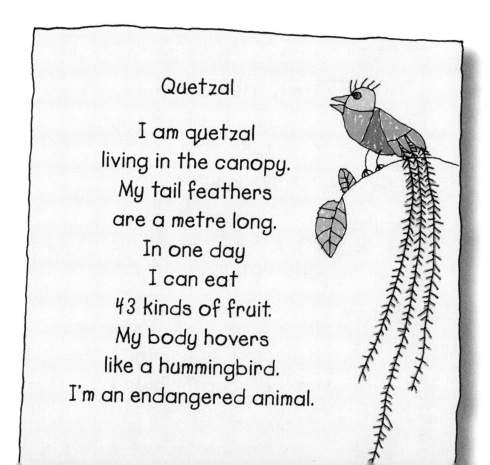

Quetzal

I am quetzal
living in the canopy.
My tail feathers
are a metre long.
In one day
I can eat
43 kinds of fruit.
My body hovers
like a hummingbird.
I'm an endangered animal.

Drawings in a Picture Book

Sometimes you can make a whole picture book. Jamie made a picture book for his all-about-me story. Each page had one or two sentences and a picture. Here is one of his pages:

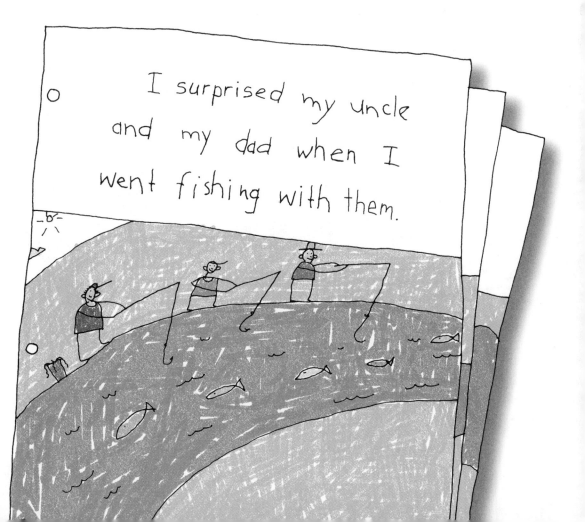

I surprised my uncle and my dad when I went fishing with them.

Binding a Book

Book Design

Books can be different shapes and sizes.

Steps to Follow

- Make a front and back cover.
- Design a title page.
- Stack all the pages between the covers.
- Put your book together with yarn, rings, staples, or string.

Book Cover and Title Page

Example Cover

Example Title Page

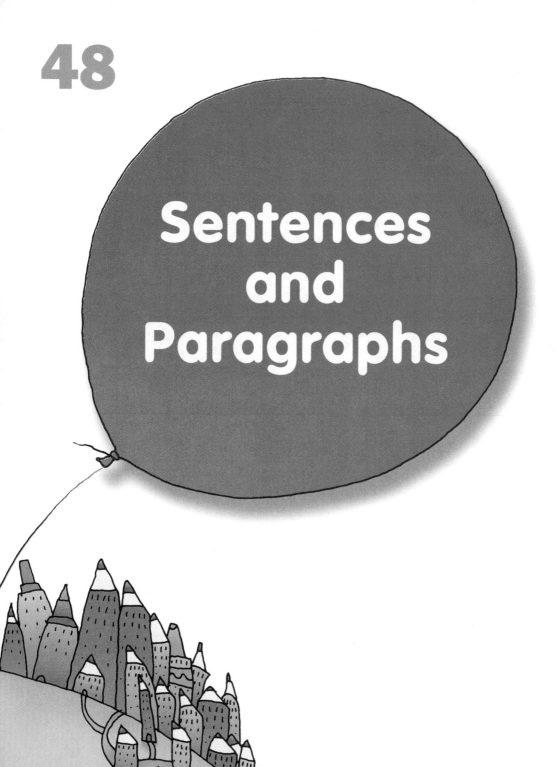

Sentences and Paragraphs

Writing Sentences

A **sentence** is a group of words that tells a complete idea. Every sentence has a naming part and a telling part.

The Naming Part	The Telling Part
Aunt Jill	works.
The boys	play in the yard.

Sentence Parts

Subject

The naming part is also called the **subject**. The subject names who or what the sentence is about.

Grandpa sings.

Verb

The telling part is also called the **verb**. The verb usually tells what the subject is doing.

Grandpa sings.

Other Parts

We usually add words to the subject or verb to make the idea clearer.

Grandpa sings in the shower.

Subject/Verb Agreement

The <u>subject</u> and <u>verb</u> must go together in a sentence.

Singular subjects go with singular verbs (Singular means "one.")

Olga loves milk.

Plural subjects go with plural verbs. (Plural means "more than one.")

My cousins love juice.

Sentence Problem

Try not to run too many sentences together using the words "and then."

Too many "and then's":

Minu ate his lunch really fast and then he jumped up and then he ran outside.

Better:

Minu ate his lunch really fast. Then he jumped up and ran outside.

Writing Longer Sentences

Do you know how to write longer sentences? You can combine two or three shorter ones.

Two sentences:
>Polar bears swim fast.
>Polar bears catch fish.

One longer sentence:
>**Polar bears swim fast and catch fish.**

The next page shows you how to combine sentences.

Combine Subjects

Two sentences:

Foxes live near the North Pole.
Wolves live near the North Pole.

Longer sentence with two subjects:

Foxes and wolves live near the North Pole.

Combine Verbs

Three sentences:

Penguins dive in water.
They leap in water.
They paddle in water.

Longer sentence with three verbs:

Penguins dive, leap, and paddle in water.

You can combine other words, too.

Walruses look big, fat, and sleepy.

Writing Paragraphs

Writing is many things. It is describing a subject or giving information. It is sharing a story or giving reasons.

Sharing and Telling

You can do all of these things in a paragraph. This chapter shows you how to write a describing paragraph, plus much more.

What Is a Paragraph?

A **paragraph** is three or more sentences about the same subject. All paragraphs have a beginning, a middle, and an ending.

Beginning

The first sentence is called the **topic sentence**. It names the subject. (The first sentence in a paragraph is indented.)

Middle

The middle sentences are called the **body**. They tell about the subject.

Ending

The last sentence is called the **closing sentence**. It gives an interesting idea about the subject.

Reading model paragraphs helps you write them. You can get started by reading the model on the next page.

Student MODEL

In this model, Michael decribes his favourite sandwich.

My Best Sandwich

Topic Sentence

Toasted cheese sandwiches are great.

Body

They smell buttery and look golden brown. When you bite into one, you can see the melted yellow cheese. Toasted cheese sandwiches taste crunchy on the outside and creamy in the middle.

Closing Sentence

I could eat one every day!

Writing a Describing Paragraph

1 PLAN

Pick a Subject

Pick a person, place, or thing to describe.

Collect Ideas

List ideas about your subject. How does it look, sound, or smell?

2 WRITE

Write the Three Parts

Name your subject in the topic sentence. Tell about it in the middle sentences. End with a closing idea that's interesting.

Check Your First Draft

3

REVISE

* Do all of your sentences describe the subject?
* Are your sentences in the best order?

Check for Errors

4

CHECK

Check your sentences for capital letters, punctuation, and spelling. Then write a neat final copy.

Remember to indent the first line in your paragraph.

More Models

Giving Information

In this paragraph, Kumal gives important information about plants and their roots.

Plant Roots

Topic Sentence Plant roots do their work underground. They spread out to find water. They also soak up minerals to make **Body** the plant healthy. When it rains hard, roots keep the plant standing. A plant would **Closing Sentence** die without roots.

Sharing a Story

In this paragraph, Kala shares a story about visiting a park.

Park Adventure

Topic Sentence

My dad and I went to Blue Hills Park. We hiked to the top of a big hill above the clouds! Then we explored Treasure

Body

Cave. It was scary and dark inside. Later, we saw three fat raccoons. We

Closing Sentence

had a lot of fun and will visit the park again!

Giving Reasons

In this paragraph, Dee Dee gives reasons why her aunt is so special.

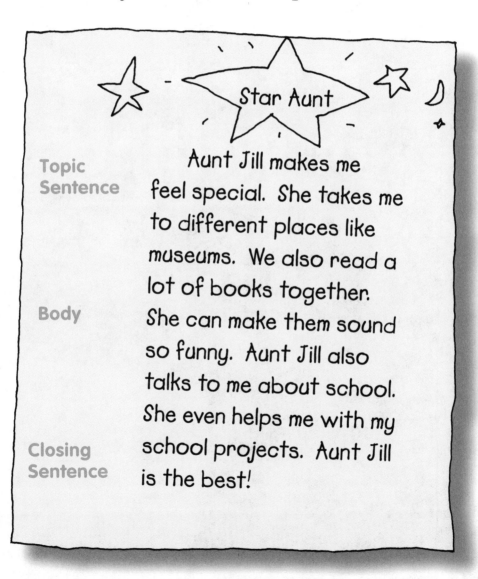

Star Aunt

Topic Sentence

Aunt Jill makes me feel special. She takes me to different places like museums. We also read a lot of books together.

Body

She can make them sound so funny. Aunt Jill also talks to me about school. She even helps me with my

Closing Sentence

school projects. Aunt Jill is the best!

The FORMS of Writing

64

Personal Writing

Writing in Journals

In a **journal**, you can write about how you feel and what you think. It is your very own writing place!

A Present a Day

Josh says, "Writing in a journal is like giving yourself a present every day!" Josh is ready to help you start your own journal. Just follow along.

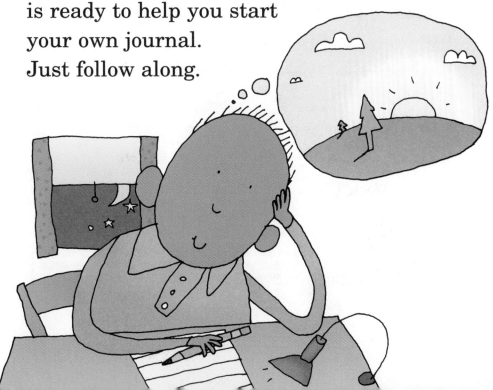

Journal-Writing TIPS

WRITE in your journal every day.

KEEP your eyes and ears open for ideas.

DON'T WORRY about your spelling, but try to write neatly.

DRAW pictures whenever you want to because drawing helps you think.

REREAD your journal a lot. You will get good ideas for other writing you do.

Ideas for Journal Writing

Josh writes about events.

September 6
   We performed our poem today. Everybody liked how we jumped up when we said the last line—"I just want to grow up!" The kids were surprised.

Josh writes about learning.

January 30
Here are some good habits
we're learning about in school.
- eat healthful foods
- play a lot
- relax
Another idea is
to be nice to other kids!

He also writes about his reading.

March 8
I want to write a book just
like Uncle Henry's Dinner Guests.
It's the funniest book I have
ever read. I want to be able
to write a book and make
people laugh.

Writing Friendly Notes

You can write notes to a lot of people. You can write to your friends, your mom, or your dad. You can even write notes to your teacher. People like to get friendly notes. It tells them that you care.

Notes Are Easy

To get started, write a note to a friend. Put it in a special place where he or she will find it. You may soon get a note back!

Cool Ideas for Notes

Tell Something You Know

Dear Josie,

An anteater eats 30000 ants a day. We need one at our house.

Ha ha,
Tanya

Send Good Wishes

Dear Joe,

I'm sorry you broke your leg. We miss you. I hope you'll be back soon.

Your friend,
Eric

Say Thank You

Dear Uncle Mike,

Thank you for the calculator. You always know what I need! Now I can check my math homework.

Love,
Sarah

Share a Message

Dear Mom,
My mom works hard.
My mom is true-blue.
My mom likes jokes.
And I do, too.
Love,
Latisha
Do you know what the wolf's mom said to him?
I'll tell you at dinner!

Fun Note Ideas

Here are two ways to have fun with notes.

Cut out a shape for your note.

Lee,
Meet me at the park after school.
Saul

Add a picture to your note.

Linda,
My mom says you can stay over on Friday.
We can have pizza.
Ask your mom.

Beth

Writing Friendly Letters

Friendly letters are a lot like friendly notes. But friendly letters travel! They can reach friends and relatives far away.

Reaching Out

Write a letter and put a smile on someone's face. John did! Read his letter on the next page. Then we will help you write your own letter.

Student MODEL

Friendly letters have five parts. The parts are marked in this letter.

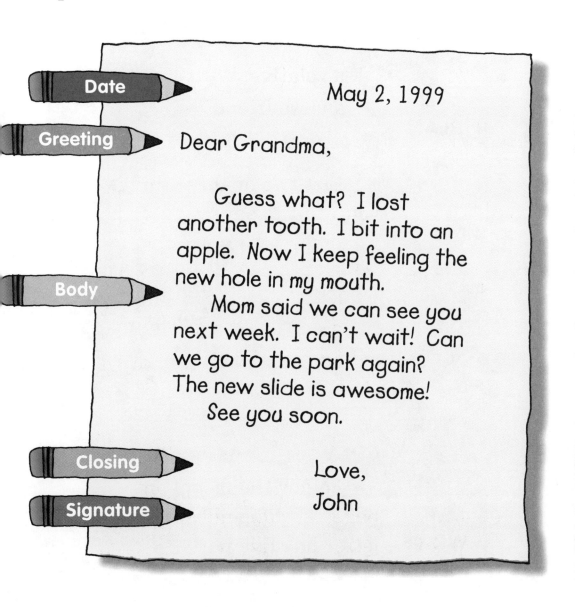

Date

May 2, 1999

Greeting

Dear Grandma,

Body

Guess what? I lost another tooth. I bit into an apple. Now I keep feeling the new hole in my mouth.

Mom said we can see you next week. I can't wait! Can we go to the park again? The new slide is awesome!

See you soon.

Closing

Love,

Signature

John

Steps in Writing a Friendly Letter

1
PLAN

Pick Someone to Write To
* a relative
* a close friend

List Ideas

List two or three things you want to say.

I lost my tooth.
We are coming
to visit.
Can we go
to the park?

2
WRITE

Put Your Ideas on Paper

Follow the model on page 73. Remember that a letter has five parts.

3

REVISE

Check Your First Draft

* Did you say all of the important things?
* Did you remember the five parts of a letter?

4

CHECK

Check for Errors

✔ Check your sentences for capital letters.
✔ Check for punctuation and spelling.
✔ Make sure your letter looks nice.

To send your letter, see pages 100-101 for help.

Writing All-About-Me Stories

All-about-me stories tell about things that happen to you. They can be funny or surprising. They can be long or short. They can be old or new.

Getting Started

You can read an all-about-me story on the next page. Then we'll show you how to write your own story to share.

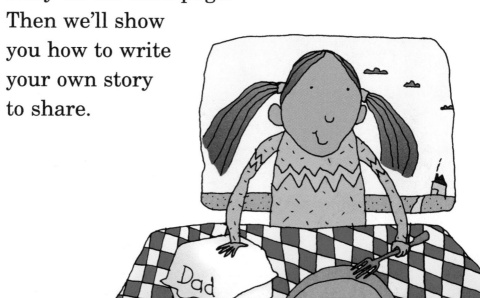

Dad

Student MODEL

Keeping the Dressing

Last summer I made my sister really mad. My grandmother gave us money to eat in the dining car on the train. I ate turkey. I asked the waiter to wrap up the dressing. I said, "I don't like dressing, but my dad does."

My sister is 12. She says she will never go to a restaurant with me again. She says nobody wants old dressing. But my dad ate it.

Susan

Steps in Writing an All-About-Me Story

PLAN

List Ideas

List two or three things that happened to you.

I broke *my arm* on vacation.

I ate dinner on a train.

I lost *my cat.*

Choose a Story Idea

Pick one idea from your list to write about.

Talk About Your Idea

Tell your story out loud to a friend.

2 WRITE

Start with a Bang
Here is Susan's first sentence:

"Last summer I made my sister really mad."

Write the Rest of the Story
Tell all of the parts.

3 REVISE

Read Your First Draft
Did you forget anything?

Make Changes
Add any missing parts.

4 CHECK

Check for Errors
Check your sentences for end punctuation, capital letters, and spelling. Write a neat final copy.

Subject Writing

Writing About Books

Reading a good book is fun. Sharing your ideas about the book can be fun, too. You can share your ideas in a book review.

Getting Started

This chapter will help you write a book review. It includes two models for you to read and writing guidelines for you to follow.

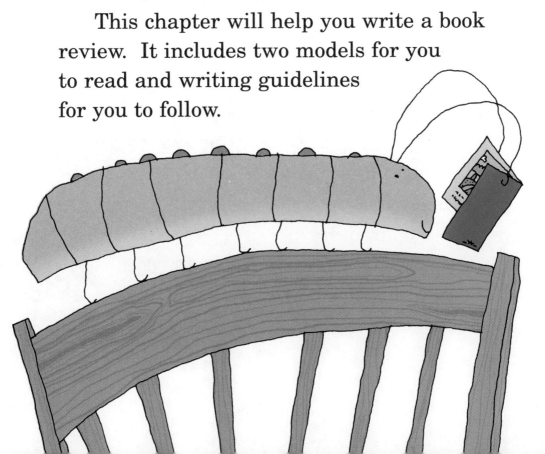

MODEL Book Review

Here is Teresa's review of a book with a make-believe story. Each paragraph answers a main question.

1. What is the book about?
2. Why do I like this book?

Grandpa's Visit

Grandpa's Visit is a book by Ricardo Keens-Douglas. It is about a boy called Jeremy who likes computers. His Grandpa comes to visit and doesn't know anything about computers. Grandpa crashes the computer.

This book is funny. I liked the way Jeremy and his family find other things to do to have fun.

MODEL **Book Review**

Here is Anton's review of a true story. Each paragraph answers a main question.

1. What is the book about?

2. Why do I like this book?

Cheryl's Potlatch

Cheryl's Potlatch is a book by Sheila Thompson. It is about a First Nations girl from the Carrier Nation in British Columbia. Her family is planning a potlatch to give her a Carrier Nation name. A potlatch is held to celebrate something special. Everybody gets gifts to take home.

I really liked this book. It has lots of pictures to show how to get ready for a potlatch. I liked how the story is told in English and in Cheryl's First Nations language.

Writing a Book Review

1 PLAN

Pick a Book

Choose a book that you like a lot.

Think About the Book

What happens in this book? What is the best part? (You could draw a picture.)

2 WRITE

Answer Two Main Questions

* What is the book about?
* Why do I like it?

3 REVISE

Check Your First Draft

* Did you answer the two questions?
* Did you include all of the important ideas in your answers?

4 CHECK

Check for Errors

Check your sentences for capital letters, punctuation, and spelling. Then write a neat final copy.

Making Counting Books

Counting jingles are fun to say:

One, two, buckle my shoe.
Three, four, shut the door.
Five, six, pick up sticks. . . .

And counting books are fun to make!

Numbers Plus!

Counting books use numbers . . . of course. There are special words and pictures to go with the numbers, too.

one spot
two spots
old spot
new spots

Student MODEL

Here is the first page in Shari's counting book called *Circus Fun.* (She counts by 2's.)

Here is the second page in Shari's counting book.

4 Crazy Clowns

Shari has chosen words that begin with the same sound (Crazy Clowns). This makes her book fun to read.

Making a Counting Book

1 PLAN

Pick a Number Pattern

* 1, 2, 3, 4, . . .
* 2, 4, 6, 8, . . .
* 5, 10, 15, 20, . . .

Pick a Subject

What will you write and draw about?

Shari picked the circus.

Plan Your Book

What types of ideas will you put on each page?

Shari named different circus performers.

2 WRITE

State Your Ideas

* Use special words:
  2 Amazing Acrobats

* Or use sentences:
  Two acrobats did flips.

Draw Your Pictures

3 REVISE

Check Your Work

* Do all of the numbers fit the pattern?

* Did you use the best words and pictures?

4 CHECK

Check for Errors

✔ Look carefully for spelling errors. Then make a neat final copy of your book.

Writing with Numbers and Rhyme

Here's how Stephen used numbers and rhyme in a fun way.

His First Step ● He made two lists.

Numbers	Rhyming Words
one	bun, fun, run, sun
two	boo, new, zoo
three	bee, knee, see, tree

His Second Step ● Then he wrote two sentences for each number.

Numbers and Rhyme

First there's one.
Get ready for fun.

Next comes two.
Let's go to the zoo.

Writing News Stories

Students in Room 20 wanted to share their writing with other classes. So they made a newspaper called the *Record*. It is filled with stories about school life.

Read All About It!

You can read one of the stories on the next page. Then you can learn how to write your own news story.

MODEL News Story

THE RECORD

New Food Plan ❶

by Beth Cramer ❷

❸ We now have two choices for hot lunch.

❹ The cooks keep a record of the most popular choices. So far, pizza is the first choice. Hot dogs are second.

Ms. Hunt is our food director. She said, "We want students to eat all of their food and enjoy it." ❺

Parts of a News Story

❶ The **headline** names the story.

❷ The **byline** shows the author.

❸ The **beginning** gives the most important idea.

❹ The **middle** tells more about the story.

❺ The **ending** gives the reader an idea to remember.

Writing a News Story

1 PLAN

List Ideas

List two or three important events:
- *your class play*
- *the new lunch plan*

Pick One Idea

Choose the best idea for your news story.

Collect Facts

Here are ways to collect facts about your idea:

* Talk to people about it.
* Read about it.
* Watch it in action.

2 WRITE — Write the Story

* Give the most important idea in the first sentence.
* Give other facts in the middle.
* End with an interesting idea.

3 REVISE — Check the First Draft

Did you include all the facts?

4 CHECK — Check for Errors

Check your story for spelling, capital letters, and periods. Write a neat final copy.

Writing Business Letters

Grownups write business letters all the time. They send for information. They order things. They try to solve problems.

Sending Out

You can learn to write business letters, too. Then you can send for information for school and do other neat things. We will show you how in this chapter.

Zoo Director
Mytown, ON
K1A 2B2

POS

Letter-Writing TIPS

KNOW why you are writing your letter.

- Do you need information for school?
- Do you want to join a club?
- Do you want to order something?

FIND out who to write to.

STATE your ideas clearly and neatly.

SOUND polite and thankful. In most cases, you will be writing to a grown-up.

FOLLOW the form for a business letter and for the address on an envelope. (See pages 98-100.)

USE your best handwriting. (If you can, type your letter on a computer.)

CHECK the letter for errors before sending it.

Six Parts of a Business Letter

1 Heading: Give your address and the date.

2 Inside Address: Write the name and address of the person or company you are writing to.

3 Salutation: Use a title, or **Ms.** for women and **Mr.** for men.

Dear Officer Friendly:

Dear Ms. Cheng:

4 Body: Explain what you need.

5 Closing: Use **Sincerely** followed by a comma (,).

6 Signature: Write your name under the closing.

MODEL Business Letter

1 609 Market Street
Baytown, ON K1A 2B3
March 30, 1999

2 Officer Friendly
Baytown Police Department
100 Main Street
Baytown, ON K1A 2B3

3 Dear Officer Friendly:

My name is Michael Sanders, and I
am in Grade 3. We are going to
study bike safety. It will be next
week.

4
I think you know a lot about bike
safety. Please send me your
information. It is my job for the class.

Thank you.

5 Sincerely,

6 Michael Sanders

Sending Your Letter

Addressing the Envelope

- Print neatly.
- Use the post office abbreviations for provinces and streets. (See pages 258-259).
- Put your address in the top left-hand corner.
- Put the stamp in the top right-hand corner.

MICHAEL SANDERS
609 MARKET ST
BAYTOWN, ON K1A 2B3

CANADA

OFFICER FRIENDLY
BAYTOWN POLICE DEPARTMENT
100 MAIN STREET
BAYTOWN, ON K1A 2B3

Folding Your Letter

- Fold your letter into three equal parts.
- Put your letter into the envelope. Then seal the envelope.
- Check the address and stamp.
- Mail your letter!

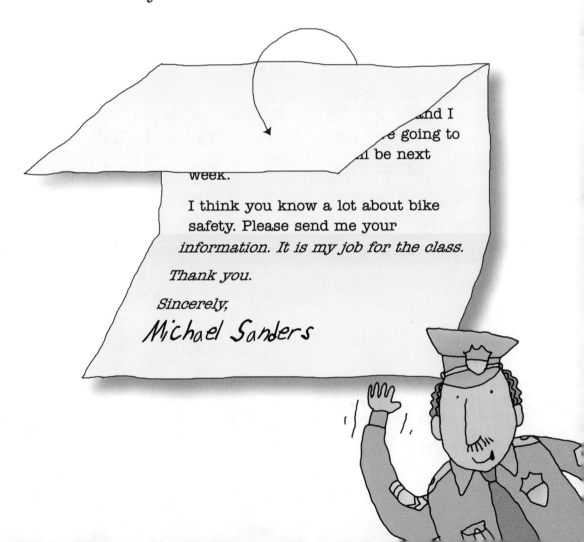

...nd I ...e going to ...l be next week.

I think you know a lot about bike safety. Please send me your information. It is my job for the class.

Thank you.

Sincerely,

Michael Sanders

Writing Directions

Everyone is good at something. You may be good at hitting a softball. Or you may make the best peanut butter and jam sandwich. Yum!

Step-by-Step

In this chapter, we will show you how to write **directions**. Then you can explain how your skill is done. Or you can explain how to get to a special place.

Two Kinds of Directions

Making a PB & J Sandwich

It's easy to make a peanut butter and jam sandwich. First, spread peanut butter on one piece of bread. Then, spread jam on the other piece. Next, put the two pieces of bread together. Keep the peanut butter and jam on the inside. Last, cut the sandwich in half and start eating!

How to Get to the Nurse's Office

1. Go out of our classroom and turn left.
2. Walk to the stairs and go down.
3. Turn right at the bottom of the stairs.
4. Walk a long way down the hall.
5. Stop at Room 104, the nurse's office.

Writing a Set of Directions

1 PLAN

Pick a Subject

Choose something you like to do or make. (Or choose a special place to go.)

Think About It

* What will you say in your directions?
* What steps will you give?

2 WRITE

Write the Directions

* Use time words like *first* and *then* to make your directions clear.
* Or use numbers before each step.

Check the Directions

3
REVISE

* Did you include all the steps?
* Are the steps in the right order?

Check for Errors

4
CHECK

Check your sentences for spelling, capital letters, and periods. Then write a neat copy of your directions to share.

You can add pictures to your directions, too.

Making Posters

Posters are like BIG notes. Some posters tell about special events. They tell where and when an event is going to happen. Posters may also say something important about a subject.

Post a Big Note!

Study the posters on the next two pages. Then learn how to make your own.

MODEL Telling About an Event

MODEL Sharing an Idea

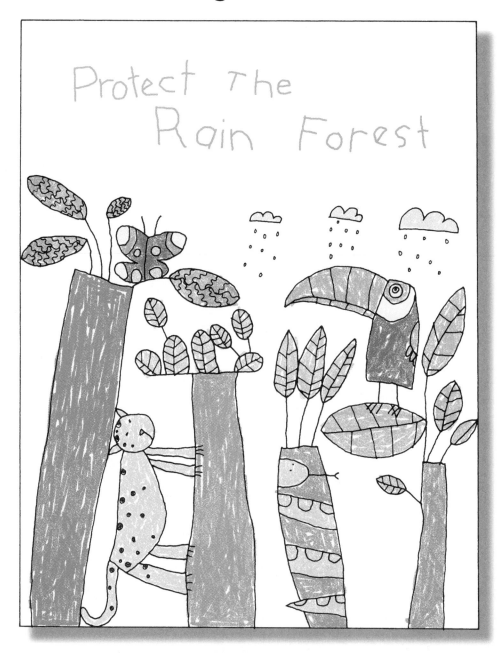

Poster-Making TIPS

A good poster needs a strong picture and just a few words. Here are some tips to follow:

GATHER all your facts.

THINK of a main idea to put in your picture.

PLAN your poster on a small piece of paper.
- Use all the space.
- Put your title in big letters.

DRAW a copy of your plan onto a large piece of paper.

SHOW your work to a classmate. Maybe your friend will give you an idea.

CHECK your spelling and facts.

COLOUR your poster.

110

Research
Writing

Using the Library

A library is packed with books. There are books about neat places and wild animals. There are books full of great stories and much more!

Looking and Learning

This chapter talks about the different kinds of books. It also shows you how to find books and how to use them. All of these ideas will help you use the library.

Learning About Library Books

Fiction Books

A **fiction book** is make-believe. The story did not really happen. The author made it up.

Look for It Fiction books have their own place in the library. They are usually found in ABC order by the author's last name.

Nonfiction Books

A **nonfiction book** is true. Nonfiction books give facts about subjects like the rain forest and airplanes.

Look for It Nonfiction books are put on the shelves in number order. They have "call numbers" printed on them. (See page 116 to learn more about this.)

Biographies

A **biography** is a true book about the life of an important person like a prime minister or an inventor.

Look for It Biographies have their own place in the library, too. They are in ABC order by the last name of the person the book is about.

Reference Books

A **reference book** has lots of facts and information. Encyclopedias and dictionaries are reference books.

Look for It Reference books have a special place in the library. Your teacher or librarian will show you where they are.

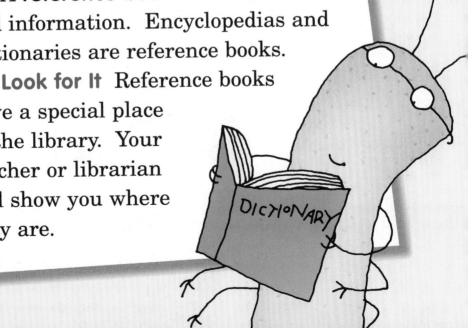

Finding Library Books

Card Catalogue

The **card catalogue** names the books in your library. A book usually has a title card, a subject card, and an author card in this catalogue. All of the cards in the catalogue are in ABC order.

Example Title Card

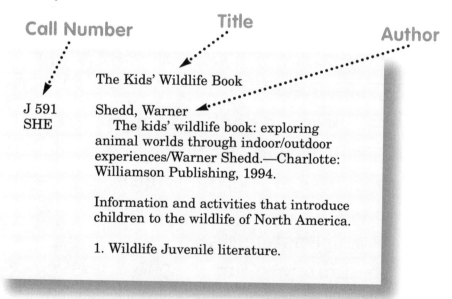

You can look in the card catalogue for a title, a subject, or an author. If a title begins with *A, An,* or *The,* look up the next word.

Computer Catalogue

Many libraries have their card catalogues on a computer. The computer shows you the same information you would find in a card catalogue. You just type in a title, an author, or a keyword. A **keyword** works like a subject card.

```
Author:       Shedd, Warner

Title:        The Kids' Wildlife Book

Published:    Charlotte: Williamson
              Publishing, 1994.

Subject:      Wildlife Juvenile litera-
ture

Call number:            Status:
J 591 SHE               Not checked out

Location:
Children's
```

Using Call Numbers

To find nonfiction books, you need to know the **call number**. *The Kids' Wildlife Book* by Warner Shedd has this call number: J591
SHE

Below, you can see where this book fits on the shelf.

J499 BRE   J552 CHE   J552 DAR   J591 SHE   J592 BRE

GOOD POINT

Always ask your librarian or teacher for help if you cannot find a book. Either one can help you become "library smart"!

Using Nonfiction Books

Nonfiction books are easier to use when you understand their parts. Here are the main parts in nonfiction books.

At the Beginning

- The **title page** is the first page. It gives the book title and the author's name.
- The **table of contents** names each chapter and tells what page it starts on.

In the Middle

- The **body** is the main part of the book. It includes all of the chapters.

At the End

- The **glossary** explains special words used in the book.
- The **index** is an ABC list of all the topics in the book. It gives the page number where each topic is found.

Writing Reports

John Walker learned three things about his favourite dinosaur: *how big it was, what it ate,* and *where it lived.* Then he wrote a report about this information. You can read this report on page 123.

Finding and Sharing

Do you know how to find information about a subject? We will show you how in this chapter. We will also show you ways to report on what you find out.

Finding Information for Reports

Select a Good Subject

- Start with a large topic you are studying. It could be dinosaurs.

- List ideas about the topic that interest you. You can look in books or ask friends for ideas.

- Choose the most interesting idea to be your subject.

Think About Your Subject

- Write two or three questions you have about your subject.

- Put your questions on note cards or on a gathering grid. (See page 121 for a model grid.)

Learn About Your Subject

- You can look in many places to learn about your subject:

    books, tapes, magazines, interviews, CD's, the Internet

- Try to use more than one source of information.

- Write answers to your questions as you read and learn. Do this on note cards or on a gathering grid.

Example Note Card

What did Brachiosaurus eat?

- leaves from trees
- water plants

Using a Gathering Grid

A **gathering grid** helps you organize the information you collect about your subject.

Getting Started

USE a big piece of paper.

DRAW lines to make a grid.

WRITE your questions and answer them.

Brachiosaurus	Book	Tape and Picture Set
How big was it?	22–24 m long and 12 m high	taller than a four-storey building
What did it eat?	tree leaves	water plants

If you think of new questions or find other facts, write them on your grid.

Writing a Classroom Report

You can write about your information in a classroom report. This page will help you. Also see John's report on the next page.

Beginning   Your first paragraph should name your subject in an interesting way. John starts by asking a question. You could also give an important fact.

Middle   Use the information from your notes to write the main part. Each paragraph should answer one question.

Ending   Tell what you have learned or how you feel about the subject.

Remember to check your report for errors before you write a final copy.

MODEL Classroom Report

Brachiosaurus
by John Walker

What's the longest, tallest, and heaviest dinosaur that ever lived? It was the Brachiosaurus.

Beginning

Brachiosaurus was 22–24 m long and 12 m high. That was taller than a four-storey building! It had a long neck. It could reach the top of 12 m trees.

Brachiosaurus ate water plants and leaves from trees. It must have eaten a lot. One Brachiosaurus was as heavy as 10 elephants.

Middle

Brachiosaurus lived in the western part of North America. Maybe I'll find a fossil someday.

Ending

Example Picture

4th story
3rd story
2nd story
1st story

More Reporting Ideas

This list shows other ways to report on information. You can probably think of many more!

LIST POEM Write a poem that gives facts about your subject. (See the next page.)

STORY Write a story about your subject. (See the next page.)

POSTER Make a poster about your subject. (See pages 106-109.)

PICTURE DICTIONARY Report on your subject in a picture dictionary. (See pages 126-129.)

ORAL REPORT Tell important facts about your subject. Have pictures or examples that show your facts, too.

MODEL
List Poem

Garrett lists many facts about an ocelot in his poem.

Ocelot

I am an ocelot.
You can find me climbing
Up the trees
Trying to find my prey.
Some things I eat
Are snakes and lizards.
You can only find me
Doing this at night.
I am 122 cm long.
My big eyes help me see.

MODEL
Story

Here is the start of Lauren's story about an otter.

Carl Otter

I, Carl Otter, live in a pond. In this pond there are hundreds of animals, like snakes, ducks, frogs, fish, moose, salamanders, beavers, and, of course, otters! I love my home . . .

Making Picture Dictionaries

To make a **picture dictionary**, you need to do three things:

1. Put a set of words in ABC order.

2. Write something about each word.

3. Draw a picture for each word.

Picking a Subject

A picture dictionary can be about anything from dogs to dinosaurs to kites. This chapter will help you make your own picture dictionary.

Student MODEL

Tony did a picture dictionary about motor vehicles.   You can see some of his work on the next two pages.

MOTORCYCLE

A motorcycle has two wheels. People ride motorcycles for fun. One or two people can ride on a motorcycle.

PICKUP

A pickup has four wheels. People haul things in pickups. A pickup usually has room for two people.

Dictionary-Making TIPS

PICK a subject you really like. Here are some ideas:

> wild animals
>
> motor vehicles
>
> dinosaurs
>
> musical instruments

LIST words for your dictionary. Each word should be about the subject.

SELECT the best words. (You don't have to use all of them.)

PUT the words in ABC order.

FIND facts for each word.

SET UP your dictionary. Each page should have a word, sentences, and a picture.

CHECK your pages for spelling errors.

MAKE a final copy with a cover. (See pages 46-47 for help.)

Story
Writing

Writing Circle Stories

Jane loves circle stories. A **circle story** begins and ends in the same place. Jane thinks it's fun to figure out how the author will get back to the beginning.

Reading and Writing

One day, Jane's teacher read *If You Give a Mouse a Cookie* by Laura Numeroff. After hearing it, Jane had a great idea for a circle story. You can read it on the next page.

Student MODEL

Here is Jane's circle story:

If You Give a Kitten Some String!

If you give a kitten some string . . .
She'll play with it.
Then she'll get all tangled up!
Then she'll go in the kitchen so you can
   get her untangled!
Then she'll leave the string there
   because she's tired, and she'll lie on
   your bed!
Then she'll want you to read her a story.
Then the story will get boring, so she'll
   look for some string to play with.
And, chances are, she'll get all tangled up
   again!

Jane drew a picture for each
main idea in her story.

Story-Writing TIPS

READ more circle stories. That will help you write your own. Here are three more:

The Dark by Robert Munsch
Sadie and the Snowman by Allen Morgan
Rosie's Walk by Pat Hutchins

MAKE a map of ideas for your story. Here is the start of Jane's story map:

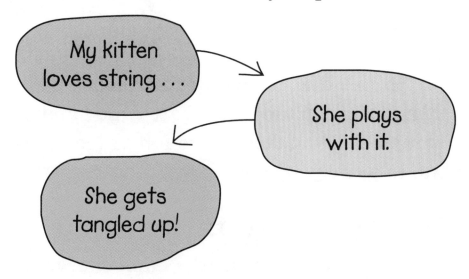

> My kitten loves string . . .
>
> She plays with it.
>
> She gets tangled up!

WRITE your story and draw your pictures.

CHECK your story for errors before you share it.

Writing Add-On Stories

Stories like "The Very Enormous Turnip" and "Stone Soup" are called add-on stories. Add-on stories are fun to read and fun to write.

The Working Parts

In an **add-on story**, the main character has a problem. One by one, different characters are added to the story. A surprise happens in the end, and the problem is solved.

Student MODEL

Here is Connie's add-on story:

Dance Steps

Connie really wanted to tap-dance. She tried, but she couldn't do it.

So she asked Karen, her baby sitter, to teach her. Karen said, "Sorry, I only know how to line-dance."

Then Connie asked her friend Lizzy. But Lizzy said, "Sorry, I only know how to square-dance."

Next, Connie asked her neighbour Mr. Cosford. But he said, "Sorry, I only know how to polka."

Connie thought she would never learn. She asked one last person, her dad. He said, "Sure, I'll teach you how to tap-dance."

So Connie and her dad danced and danced. Everyone was so surprised. No one knew her dad could tap-dance!

Writing an Add-On Story

1
PLAN

Pick a Main Character

List Story Ideas or Problems

Here is Connie's list:

choosing a pet

✔ learning to tap-dance

fixing a bike

Choose One Problem for Your Story

List Add-On Characters

Connie listed people she knew:

baby sitter   dad

Mr. Cosford   Lizzy

2 **WRITE**

Begin Your Story
Name the main character and tell about his or her problem.

Keep It Going
Add one character at a time to try to help.

3 **REVISE**

Check Your First Draft
* Did your characters say fun or interesting things?
* Did you save a surprise for the end?

4 **CHECK**

Check for Errors
Check your sentences for errors before you write a final copy.

Writing Fables

A **fable** is a story that teaches a lesson. You may know the fable about the tortoise and the hare. The slow tortoise wins a race because the hare rests. In the end, we learn this lesson: *slow but steady wins the race.*

Your Turn

You can write a fable, too. First read the model on the next page. Then we'll show you the steps.

MODEL Fable

The Wolf and the Kid

A mother goat and her kid lived in the woods. She had to go out to get some food, so she told her little kid to lock the door and not let anyone in. The wolf was hiding nearby and heard her. After she had gone, he went to the door and tapped lightly. The kid bleated, "Who's there?"

"It's your mother, sonny. Open the door," said the wolf in a high, squeaky voice.

The kid went around and peeked through the window. "You say you are my mother," said the kid, as he giggled. "You almost sound like her, too. But you look like a wolf to me!" And he left the door bolted.

Lesson: Mother knows best.

Writing a Fable

1 PLAN

List Characters

Pick one or two main characters for your fable. (See the list on the next page.)

Think About the Lesson

Which character will learn a lesson? What will the lesson be? (See the list on the next page for ideas.)

Think About the Setting

Where will your story take place? In a woods? At the beach? In a farmer's field?

Fable Characters

Fable characters are almost always animals. Here are some of the animals found in fables:

donkey	lion	rooster
fox	mouse	sheep
frog	owl	snake
goat	peacock	turtle
horse	rabbit	wolf

Fable Lessons

Here are some lessons to think about:

- Do not trust someone who only praises you.
- Little friends can be great friends.
- Be prepared.
- Don't count on something until it happens.

2 WRITE

Start Your Fable

Tell where the story takes place. Have your characters meet and talk.

Keep the Fable Going

* Show that one character has a problem or may need to learn a lesson.

* Make something happen. The characters may plan a contest or go someplace.

End Your Fable

Help the readers learn the lesson.

Use the model as a guide when you write.

3

REVISE

Share Your Fable

Ask your partner to listen for two things:

- a favourite part
- the lesson in the fable

Make Changes

Did you miss any parts? Did your partner have any questions?

4

CHECK

Check for Errors

✔ Check your fable for spelling, capital letters, and end punctuation.

✔ Then write a neat final copy.

Writing Mysteries

Follow the Clues

Samantha and Josh's whole class wrote mysteries. Read Josh's story starting on the next page. Then learn how to write your own mystery.

Student **MODEL**

The Case of the Missing Ring

The main character is named.

Once there was a scientist named Josh. He and his friend Ryan went to the library a lot.

In the library, there was a wooden sculpture. It had a shiny ring with a picture of a crow on it. Everyone thought the shiny ring was cool.

The mystery or problem is talked about.

One day Josh and Ryan met at the library. Ryan saw that the ring was gone. There were no scratches on the wood.

Ryan said, "Josh, come here."

Josh checked for fingerprints. "No fingerprints," he said to Ryan.

$\Rightarrow$

Then Josh heard a strange sound. He looked to his left and his right. Nothing was there.

The main character follows clues.

Josh saw the library's birdcage. The cage door was open, and the pet crow was gone.

He remembered there were no scratches or fingerprints. He thought about the ring. "I have solved the mystery," he thought.

The mystery is solved.

Josh looked up. There was the crow. It had the ring in its beak!

Ryan said, "Maybe the crow thought the picture on the ring was real."

Josh said, "That's right. Maybe the crow needed a friend."

Case closed.

Steps in Writing a Mystery Story

PLAN

List Problems to Solve

Here are some ideas:

- a lost key

- a missing gerbil

- a noise in the attic

Choose One Problem

Plan Your Story

* Who will solve your problem?

* What other characters will be in your story?

* Where will it take place?

2 WRITE

Start Your Story

Try to do these things:

* Introduce your main character.
* Tell about the problem.
* Let your reader know why the mystery has *got* to be solved.

Keep It Going

Put in clues for the main character to follow.

Solve the Mystery

Add a finishing touch.

Josh wrote,
"Case closed."

If you get stuck, reread Josh's mystery. See how he put his story together.

REVISE

Read Your First Draft

Ask yourself two main questions:

Did I put in some clues?

Did I solve my mystery?

Make Changes

Be sure your mystery is exciting. Have your characters speak to each other.

Indent each time someone new speaks. It will make your story easier to read.

CHECK

Check for Errors

✔ Check your sentences for capital letters, end punctuation, and spelling.

150

Poetry Writing

Writing Small Poems

The Pool

I live at the pool
in the summer.
The water is green
like a slice of Kiwi.
I flip off the diving board—
SPLASH—
a belly flop.

Every Word Counts

"The Pool" is a small poem by Clay. Writing a small poem is a fun way to tell about everyday things. Clay says, "You can say neat things without using lots of words."

Another MODEL

The words in Ginna's poem show how the beach looks and feels.

At the Beach

Waves are dark green
before the rain.
Saltwater feels warmest
after it rains.
Foamy waves look like bubbles
on root beer.
Maybe I will float and get near
big waves that will push me
onto the beach.
I'll reach. I'll reach.

by Ginna

Making Friends with Small Poems

Follow these tips when you read small poems.

READ the poem two or three times.

READ it aloud and listen to the sounds.

SHARE the poem with a partner.

COPY the poem into your notebook.

Which words help you see pictures?

Which words tell feelings?

Writing a Small Poem

PLAN

List Poem Ideas

Think of everyday things:

a toothbrush
the wind
stars
pebbles

Choose One Idea

Then list words and phrases about your idea. Anne listed words about the wind.

The wind

– feel it
– brushes my face
– blows seeds

2

WRITE

Write Your Poem

Here are some ideas to write about:

* ✳ Tell what your subject looks, smells, or sounds like.
* ✳ Tell what it does, or what you do with it.
* ✳ Tell how you feel about it.

Here are some special things to try:

✳ Use strong action words.

I **flip** off the diving board—

✳ Make comparisons.

The water is green
like a slice of kiwi.

✳ Add sound to your poem. (Try repeating consonant sounds.)

Foamy waves <u>l</u>ook <u>l</u>ike
bu<u>bb</u>les on root beer.

Anne's First Draft

Anne's draft shows she is trying to make her poem better.

The Wind

I feel the wind. It's ~~freezing~~ cold
and wants to brush my face.
I can't see the wind; ~~because~~
It's like an idea hidden
in my head.
The wind can blow
seeds and show
that rain is coming.

3 REVISE

Check Your First Draft

* Ask yourself questions:

    Have I used the best words?

    Have I made special comparisons?

* Mark where you want each line to end. Anne wanted to end her first line with the word "wind."

    I feel the wind./It's cold

4 CHECK

Check for Errors

✔ Check for spelling, capital letters, and punctuation.

✔ Then write your final copy. (See page 159 for Anne's final copy.)

158

Making Pleasing Sounds

Rhyme

Use rhyme to add sound to a poem.
Foamy waves look like
bubbles on root <u>beer</u>.
Maybe I will float and get <u>near</u>

Repeating Sounds

Try repeating words to add special
sound to a poem.
I'll reach. I'll reach.

Or try repeating consonant sounds.
Waves a<u>r</u>e da<u>r</u>k g<u>r</u>een

Onomatopoeia

This term stands for words that make a
sound. Use "sound words" in your poems.
<u>SPLASH</u>—
a belly flop.

Making Comparisons

- A **simile** makes a comparison using *like* or *as:*

  Shooting stars fall . . .
  <u>like</u> galloping horses.

- **Personification** makes a thing seem like a person:

  The wind wants to brush *my* face.

Anne's Final Copy

The Wind

I feel the wind.
It's cold
And wants to brush *my* face.
I can't see the wind.
It's like an idea
Hidden in *my* head.
The wind can blow seeds
And show that rain is coming.

Making Shape Poems

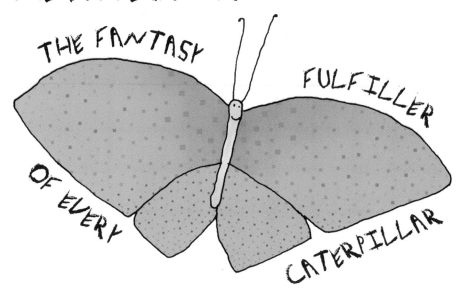

THE BUTTERFLY IS
THE FANTASY
FULFILLER
OF EVERY
CATERPILLAR

Do you like to doodle and draw?

J. Patrick Lewis does! So he makes shape poems like the butterfly above. You can, too. We will show you how.

MODEL

You can pour words *into* a shape to make a shape poem.

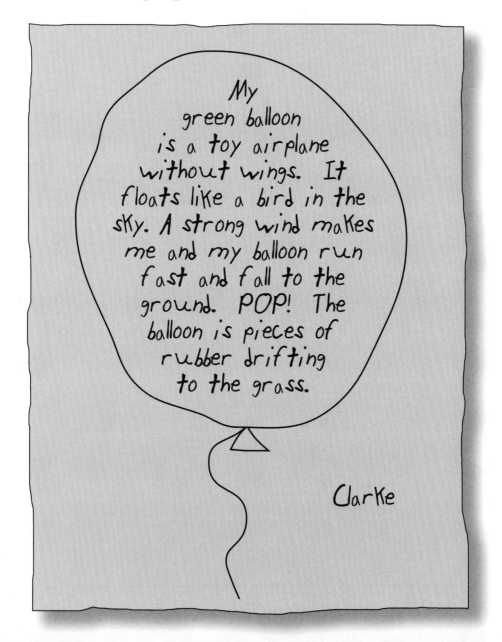

My
green balloon
is a toy airplane
without wings. It
floats like a bird in the
sky. A strong wind makes
me and my balloon run
fast and fall to the
ground. POP! The
balloon is pieces of
rubber drifting
to the grass.

Clarke

MODEL

You can also use words to *outline* a shape, as Jaime did.

Making a Shape Poem

PLAN

1

List Shapes

Think of things you like to play with or do.

football
kites
swing
blow bubbles

Choose a Shape

Make sure you can draw it.

Collect Ideas for Writing

Clarke thought about his shape, a balloon. Here are some ideas he collected.

green
floats
a bird in the sky

2 WRITE

Write Your Poem

Circle your best ideas. Put the ideas together into a poem.

Draw Your Shape

Make it big enough for your words.

Put Your Poem and Shape Together

Write your poem either inside the shape or around it.

3 REVISE

Read Your First Draft

* **Ask yourself:** Do my ideas tell about my shape?

* **Ask a friend:** What do you see when you read my poem?

4 CHECK

Check for Errors

Check for spelling, capital letters, and punctuation. Then make a neat final copy of your poem to share.

Four More Poem Ideas

ABC Poem

An **ABC poem** uses parts of the alphabet to make a funny list poem.

All
Bubbles
Can
Dance
Easily

Diamond Poem

To write a **diamond poem**, follow a syllable pattern. (Lines two and six name the subject.)

Cold	(one syllable)
winter	(two syllables)
warm knit cap	(three syllables)
mittens, sweater	(four syllables)
long red scarf	(three syllables)
winter	(two syllables)
Fun	(one syllable)

Name Poetry

A **name poem** is made by using the letters of a name or a word to begin each line.

Cute   Sunny
Happy   Planting
Red hair   Rainy
Interesting   Insects
Silly   Nests
                Gardening

Tongue Twisters

The words in a **tongue twister** begin with the same letter or sound. Say the words really fast and feel your tongue twist! Here are two examples:

Caramel Corn
Crispy, Crunchy, Creamy, Candy

Nosey Nick
Nick knotted ninety-nine noses.

The
TOOLS
of Learning

Reading Skills

Reading Graphics

Some pictures are just fun to look at. Other pictures give information. Pictures that give information are called **graphics**.

Picture Perfect

This chapter will help you read four kinds of graphics: **signs, diagrams, tables,** and **bar graphs**.

Reading Signs

A **sign** tells something important.

Clues for Understanding

- Look for letters or words on the sign.

- Look for a slash. It means "no" or "not."

  This sign means "no bicycles."

- Look at the colour of the sign.

  RED may mean "stop" or "don't."

  YELLOW may mean "be careful."

  GREEN may mean "go here."

Reading Diagrams

A **diagram** shows the parts of something or how something moves or changes.

Light Moving Through a Prism

light →

prism

red
orange
yellow
green
blue
indigo
violet

Clues for Understanding

- Look at the parts and then the whole diagram.
- Read the labels.
- Look at any arrows or pointer lines. They show how something moves or changes.

Reading Tables

A **table** is a good way to sort things.

Books I Have Read

Headings

Name of Book	Fiction	Nonfiction
Why Do Stars Twinkle? and other nighttime questions		X
The Fishing Summer	X	
Gruntle Piggy Takes Off	X	

Clues for Understanding

- Use the title to see what the table is about.
- Read the headings.
- Read across each row.

Reading Bar Graphs

A **bar graph** helps you show how many.

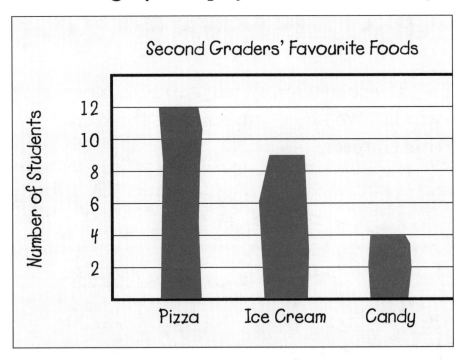

Second Graders' Favourite Foods

Number of Students: 12, 10, 8, 6, 4, 2

Pizza   Ice Cream   Candy

Clues for Understanding

- Read the title to see what the table is about.
- Read the labels at the bottom of the bars.
- Read the scale at the side of the graph. It shows how many.

Reading New Words

There are many ways to read new words. We show you some of them in this chapter.

LOOK for clues.

Read the whole sentence, but skip the word you don't know. Then think of a word that would make sense and sound right.

The **letters** in the word and the **pictures** and **ideas** on the page will help you.

LOOK for parts you know.

If you can read the word **cat**, you can read . . .

cattle   catch

If you can read **amp**, you can read . . .

camp   ramp   stamp

 Words like *camp* and *ramp* are in the same family. They have the same vowel and ending letters.

LOOK for sounds.

When you sound out a word, you try to say the word little by little.

To sound out "map," say . . .

/m/ /mă/ map

To sound out "bake," say . . .

/b/ /bā/ bake

LOOK for syllables.

Some words are too long to sound out! You need to divide them into **syllables**. Here are two ways to divide words:

Between double consonants

yel • low   ap • ple

Between two different consonants

pic • ture   sham • poo

LOOK for prefixes, suffixes, and root words.

Long words may include the root plus a prefix, a suffix, or both.

		prefix	root	suffix
unpack	=	un +	pack	
dishes	=		dish +	es
returning	=	re +	turn +	ing

L**OO**K for compound words.

Big words may be made up of two smaller words. These big words are called **compound words**.

football = foot + ball

backpack = back + pack

grasshopper = grass + hopper

If you still can't read the word, ask for help.

Reading to Understand

Funny stories make you laugh. Special poems make you feel good. And interesting fact books make you a little smarter!

Planning to Learn

This chapter will help you read fact books. Each page lists a new plan that will help you read, learn, and remember.

Preview and Predict

Think about your reading before you start. Then you will be ready to learn! Here is a plan to follow:

PREVIEW

Look at the title, bold words, and pictures. What do they tell you about the subject?

PREDICT

What do you think you will learn? What questions do you have about the subject?

GOOD POINT

Make sure to think about the subject *while* you read, and *after* you read. Did you find answers to your questions?

<u>K</u>now <u>W</u>ant <u>L</u>earn

A KWL (Know Want Learn) chart will help you think and learn when you read. Here is how to set up your KWL chart:

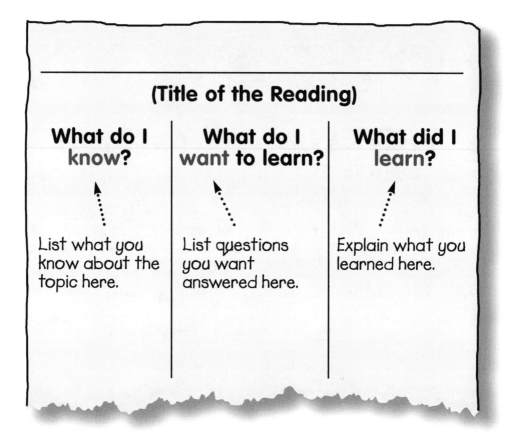

(Title of the Reading)

What do I know?	What do I want to learn?	What did I learn?
List what you know about the topic here.	List questions you want answered here.	Explain what you learned here.

TIP

Fill in the first two columns *before* you read. Fill in the last column *after* you read.

Retelling

Tell a classmate or your teacher about your reading. Talking, or retelling, helps show what you have learned. These questions will help you get started:

- What is the most important thing you learned?
- What other things did you learn?
- Are there pictures you'd like to show?

You can do your "retelling" on paper, too. Just write down all of the things you learned.

Mapping

Mapping, or clustering, helps you keep track of the main ideas in your reading. Here is a map for a book chapter about plants. (The name of the chapter is in the middle circle.)

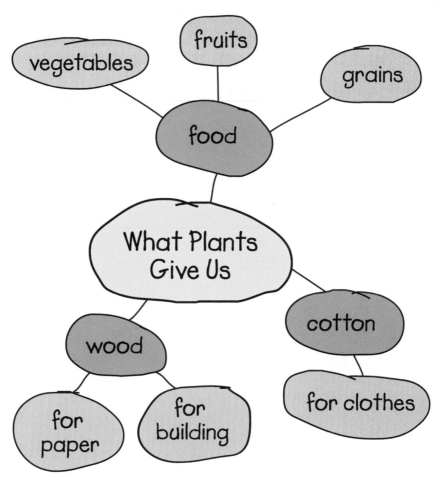

Drawing to Learn

Drawing pictures about your reading is a lot of fun. It also shows what you have learned! Sam read about animal houses. He drew pictures about this topic.

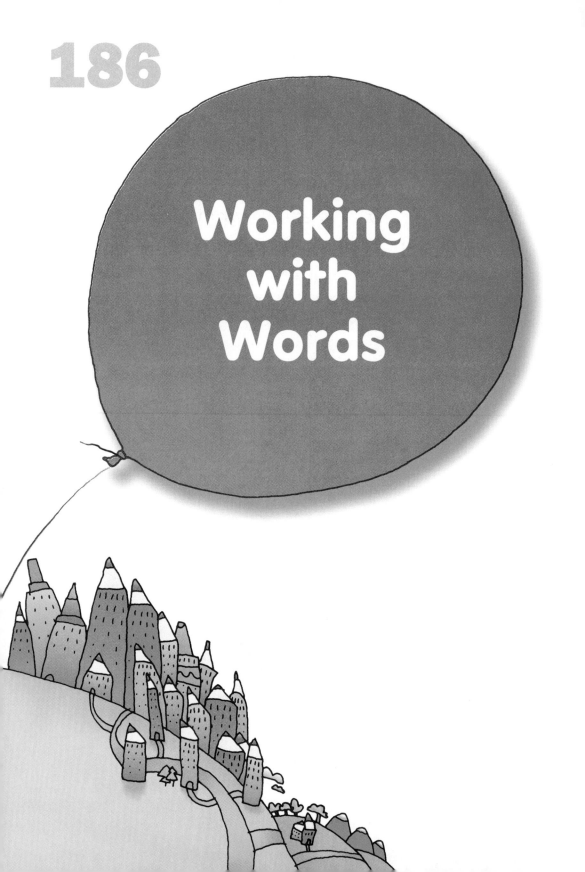

Working with Words

Using Phonics

Do you know your consonant and vowel sounds? They can help you learn new words in your reading. They can also help you spell words in your writing.

Sounding Out

This chapter is your guide to phonics. It gives examples of the basic consonant and vowel sounds. Check here when you need help with "sounding out."

Consonant Sounds

butterfly

cup cereal

duck

fish

girl gem

hat

jacket

kite

ladybug

mouse

nest

penguin

quilt

rocket

socks

turtle

vase

wagon

box

yarn

zipper

Using Consonant Blends

Consonant blends are two or more consonants that come together. Each letter keeps its own sound. Here are the basic consonant blends:

r blends   **brush, cry, drip, frog grass, pretty, trip**

l blends   **blue, cloud, flag glass, play, slide**

s blends   **skip, smile, snap spot, star, swing scrap, spring, straw**

ending blends   **band, pink, desk went, must**

Using Consonant Digraphs

Consonant digraphs are two consonant letters that come together and have one sound. Here are the basic consonant digraphs:

ch   chair, lunch, kitchen

gh   enough, laughter

ph   phone, elephant

th   this, thin, bath

wh   wheel, what

ng   sing, rang, hanger

Short Vowel Sounds

ă alligator

ĕ eggs

ĭ igloo

ŏ octopus

ŭ umbrella

Using Short Vowels

Most words with short vowel sounds have this pattern:

consonant - vowel - consonant

short ă   cat   fat   bag

short ĕ   get   bed   men

short ĭ   pin   hill   big

short ŏ   hot   pop   fox

short ŭ   rug   duck   fun

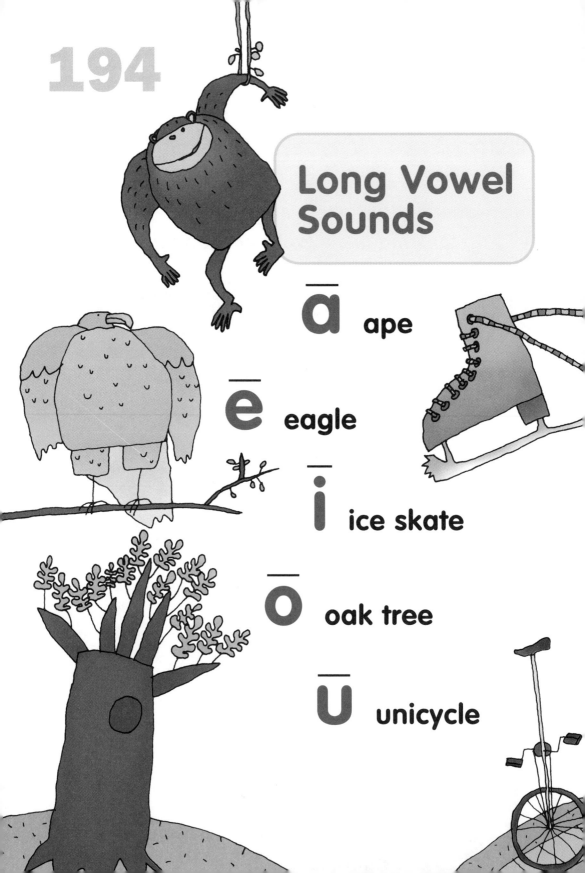

Long Vowel Sounds

$\bar{a}$ ape

$\bar{e}$ eagle

$\bar{i}$ ice skate

$\bar{o}$ oak tree

$\bar{u}$ unicycle

Using Long Vowels

Words with long vowel sounds have many different patterns.

long ā   game   train   day

long ē   meat   street   Pete

long ī   time   pie   my   night

long ō   boat   hope   go

long ū   mule   suit   Sue

Sometimes "y" is a vowel, like at the end of "fun<u>y</u>" and "fl<u>y</u>."

Using R-Controlled Vowels

Vowels followed by the letter "r" have special sounds.

ar	barn, are, cart
or	fork, more, for
er	fern, person, were
ir	bird, fir, girl
ur	curl, hurt, burn

Sometimes /er/, /ir/, and /ur/ can sound the same.

Using Diphthongs

Diphthongs (*say* dif′-thongs) are two vowel sounds that come together. They make a new sound.

oy/oi   **toy, point, coin**

ou/ow   **out, round, cow**

The same diphthong sound can have different spellings.

- You can hear **/ou/** in loud and town.

- You can hear **/oy/** in words like boy and oil.

Making New Words

The word "paint" is a root or base word. You can make "paint" into a new word by adding a word part.

A **prefix** is a part you add to the beginning of a root or base word.

re + paint = repaint

A **suffix** is a part you add to the end of a root or base word.

paint + ing = painting

Making New Words with Prefixes

The prefix **re** means "again."

re + build = rebuild

re + tell = retell

re + tie = retie

The prefix **un** means "not."

un + button = unbutton

un + happy = unhappy

un + sure = unsure

The prefix **tri** means "three."

tri + angle = triangle

tri + cycle = tricycle

tri + colour = tricolour

Making New Words with Suffixes

The suffix **ed** means "past."

call + ed = called

play + ed = played

ski + ed = skied

The suffix **er** can mean "a person who does something."

farm + er = farmer

sing + er = singer

teach + er = teacher

The suffix **ing** means "doing or acting."

catch + ing = catching

read + ing = reading

walk + ing = walking

More Prefixes

bi (meaning "two")
<u>bi</u>cycle (a two-wheeled vehicle)

ex (meaning "out")
<u>ex</u>it (to go out)

sub (meaning "under")
<u>sub</u>marine (an underwater ship)

More Suffixes

er (meaning "more")
slow<u>er</u> (more slow)

est (meaning "most")
slow<u>est</u> (most slow)

ly (meaning "in some way")
slow<u>ly</u> (in a slow way)

s, es (meaning "more than one, plural")
balloon<u>s</u> (more than one balloon)
box<u>es</u> (more than one box)

Making Contractions

A **contraction** is a shorter word made from one or two longer words. An apostrophe (') shows that one or more letters are left out.

Waldo doesn't stop playing. He's a musical monkey!

cannot	**can't**	is not	**isn't**
could not	**couldn't**	it is	**it's**
did not	**didn't**	should not	**shouldn't**
do not	**don't**	they are	**they're**
does not	**doesn't**	was not	**wasn't**
has not	**hasn't**	we are	**we're**
have not	**haven't**	we have	**we've**
he is	**he's**	will not	**won't**
I am	**I'm**	would not	**wouldn't**
I have	**I've**	you are	**you're**
I will	**I'll**	you have	**you've**

Using a Dictionary

A **dictionary** is a book that explains what words mean. The words in dictionaries are listed in the same order as the alphabet.

Here are some things you might find on a dictionary page:

Guide Words: These are the words at the top of a page. They tell you where you are in the alphabet.

Spelling: The dictionary shows the correct spelling of each word.

Meaning: The meaning helps you understand the word.

Sentence: The word is sometimes used in a sentence to make the meaning very clear.

MODEL

guide words

runner ◄ ► **rye**

runner (run′ ər) *n.* **1.** the long, narrow part on which a sled or an ice skate slides. **2.** a person who runs. **3.** an athletic shoe designed for running.

runner

runner-up (run′ ər up′) *n.* the person who finishes in second or third place in a race or contest. *pl.* **runners-up.**

runt (runt) *n.* the smallest and weakest animal born in a litter.

runway (run′ wā′) *n.* a wide, long concrete path for airplanes to take off from and land on. *pl.* **runways.**

rural (rūr′ əl) *adj.* having to do with the country, not the city: *Many students in my school were born in rural areas.*

rush (rush) *n.* **1.** a sudden or hurried movement: *I'm in a rush to catch the bus.*

rusty (rus′ tē) *adj.* covered with rust: *a rusty nail; a rustier nail; the rustiest nail in the box.*

rut (rut) *n.* a deep groove made by a wheel.
 in a rut trapped in a routine: *I'm in a rut—every day seems to be the same.*

rutabaga (rū′ tə bā′ gə) *n.* a turnip with a thick skin and pale yellow, edible flesh.

rutabaga

ruthless (ruth′ lis) *adj.* having no pity; without mercy; cruel. —**ruthlessly** adv.

rye (rī) *n.* a grass plant, grown like wheat, used for making flour and as feed for animals.

Glossary

A **glossary** is like a little dictionary in the back of a book. It tells about special words used in the book.

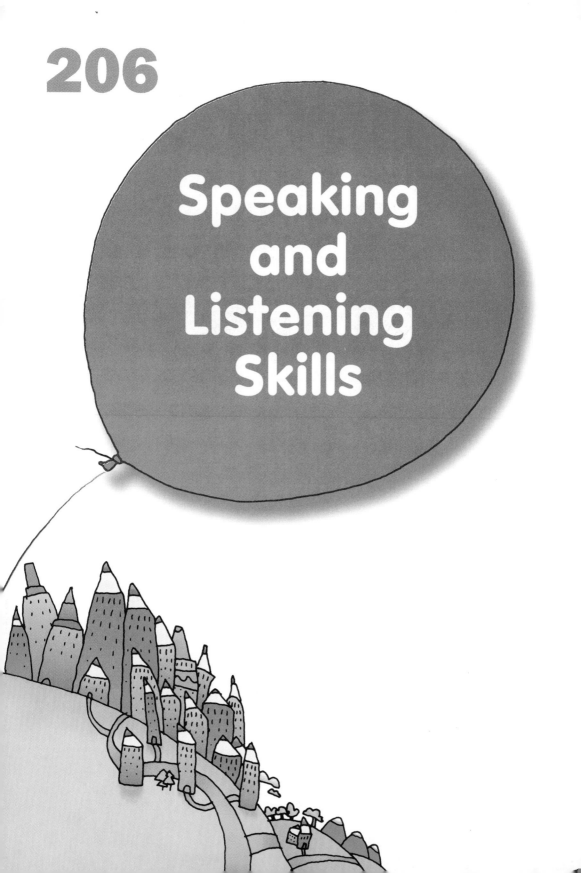

Speaking and Listening Skills

Learning to View

Most of the time, you watch TV for fun. But programs like **TV specials** help you learn things, too.

Special Shows

TV specials can be about the rain forest, dinosaurs, or almost anything. This chapter gives you a plan for watching TV specials. You will also learn about other programs and commercials.

Watching to Learn

Before the Special

- **List** questions you have about the subject.

  What is a dinosaur?

  How many dinosaurs were there?

  How do we know about them?

During the Special

- **Look** for answers to your questions.
- **Write** down key words to help you remember.

  What is a dinosaur?
  - a reptile

  How many dinosaurs were there?
  - more than 800 kinds   ?

  How do we know about them? ?   ?
  - experts find fossils

After the Special

Here are some things you can do after the program:

- **Think** about your questions. Did you find answers to them?
- **Talk** about the special with someone.
- **Write** about the important ideas.

> ### Dinosaurs
>
> Dinosaurs were reptiles. You can tell dinosaurs by the special way they walked. Their bodies didn't drag on the ground. There were more than 800 kinds of dinosaurs....

Talking and writing help you remember things!

Learning About TV Programs

There are two main types of TV programs. Some programs give **real** reports or show real events. Most other programs are **made-up** stories.

Shows like *Sesame Street* and *Incredible Story Studio* have some real parts and some made-up parts.

Learning About Commercials

Most **commercials** ask you to buy a product. They use bright colours and catchy words to make the product look and sound good. Here are some other things they do:

Using Famous People

Some commercials show a sports star using a product. If Gretzky drinks _____ , it must be good! (Is this always true?)

Bandwagon

A commercial may show many kids eating a new candy bar. You may want to join the group and eat one, too!

Problem Solving

Some commercials show how a product solves a problem. Maybe new soccer shoes help a player do better. So they must be good! (Is this always true?)

Learning to Listen

Ears can be a problem. They collect dirt, and they get full of wax! But ears do a lot of good things, too. For example, they help keep your hat on top of your head. And they allow you to listen.

Tuning In

Listening is a great way to learn. You listen to your parents, your teachers, and your friends. The next page will show you how to be a good listener.

How to Be a Good Listener

Look at the person who is speaking. This will help you follow the speaker.

Listen for key words. They help you remember important facts.

> **The Pacific Ocean is the biggest ocean.**
>
> **The Arctic Ocean is the smallest ocean.**

Listen for directions. They tell you what to do.

> **Read about oceans on page 17. List new words you find.**

Ask questions. When you don't understand something, ask for help.

Learning to Interview

Interviewing is a fun way to learn.
In an **interview**, you ask someone questions.
The other person answers them. This
chapter will show you how to interview.

Talking with a Doctor

Cheryl interviewed Jennifer
Miller. Dr. Miller is a vet
(animal doctor) who is deaf.
At the end of this chapter,
you will see what
Cheryl learned.

Before the Interview

- **Write** questions to ask the person. Think of questions that begin with **why**, **how**, and **what**.

    Why did you become a vet?

    How did you learn in school?

- **Set up** a time and place to meet for the interview.

- **Gather** your supplies. You need your list of questions and two sharp pencils.

During the Interview

- **Introduce** yourself.
- **Ask** your questions one at a time.
- **Listen** carefully to the answers.
- **Take** notes.

Why did you become a vet?

– always loved animals

– played with stuffed animals

How did you learn in school?

- At the end, **thank** the person for the interview.

Thank you.

After the Interview

● **Share** what you have learned.

Here is Cheryl's report from her interview.

My Interview

Jennifer Miller is a veterinarian. She is also deaf.

Dr. Miller always loved animals. When she was little, she played with stuffed animals. It was hard for Dr. Miller to learn in school. Sometimes friends took notes for her.

Are you wondering how Dr. Miller answered my questions? She can read lips. She can also talk. I really liked interviewing Dr. Miller.

Performing Stories

Have you ever wanted to perform a story? That's just what Kasey and her friends did. They read one of her stories in a reader's theatre performance.

Reader's Theatre

In reader's theatre, you don't have to learn the lines by heart. You read them! This chapter will show you how to plan and perform a story in this special way.

Planning to Perform

1 **Pick a Story** ● Choose a story with characters who talk to each other a lot.

2 **Form a Team** ● You will need a reader for each character. You will also need a narrator to read the nonspeaking parts.

3 **Mark the Speaking Parts** ● Mark what each character and the narrator will say. You could also write the story in script form. (See the next two pages for help.)

4 **Practise Your Reading**
● Decide who gets which part.
● Plan where to sit or stand.
● Practise the reading.

MODEL Story

Here is the first part of Kasey's story. On the next page, you will see her script.

The Yellow Elephant: Part 1

Once upon a time, Elmer went fishing by himself. His mom and dad said, "Don't talk to yellow elephants."

Elmer said, "OK!"

He went to his best fishing spot. He was so excited because he caught 10 fish. Then it was time to go home. On the way, he saw a yellow elephant.

The elephant said, "Hello!"

Elmer said, "My mom and dad told me not to talk to yellow elephants!"

"But I'm lost," said the elephant.

Elmer said, "OK, I will take you to my house."

"Oh, good!" said the yellow elephant.

"Now come on," said Elmer. And off they went.

MODEL Script

The Yellow Elephant: Part 1

NARRATOR: Once upon a time, Elmer went fishing by himself.

MOM AND DAD: Don't talk to yellow elephants, Elmer.

ELMER: OK, I won't.

NARRATOR: Elmer went to his best fishing spot. He was so excited because he caught 10 fish. Then it was time to go home. On the way, he saw a yellow elephant.

ELEPHANT: Hello!

ELMER: My mom and dad told me not to talk to yellow elephants!

ELEPHANT: But I'm lost.

ELMER: OK, I'll take you to my house. Come on.

ELEPHANT: Oh, good!

NARRATOR: So off they went.

To make a script, you may have to drop or change some words in the story.

Performing TIPS

Follow these tips when you are ready to perform your story:

INTRODUCE the story.

LOOK up from time to time when reading.

- Characters should look at the person they are talking to.
- The narrator should look at the audience.

USE your best outside voice.

KEEP going if someone makes a mistake.

JOIN hands and bow together at the end of the performance.

Important: Costumes are okay, as long as you keep them simple.

Next Step

Here is the second part of Kasey's story. Try writing a script for this part. Then practise and perform the whole story!

The Yellow Elephant: Part 2

"Mom! Dad!" yelled Elmer. "I have a yellow elephant!"

His mom and dad said, "Take him back where he was. He is dangerous."

"No, he isn't," said Elmer.

"Take him back," said his mom and dad.

Elmer took him back. By the time he got home, it was time to go to bed.

In the morning, he heard something. He looked outside. There was a yellow bird in a cage. He went outside and got it.

The bird whispered to him, "I am the yellow elephant," and Elmer believed him.

He asked his mom and dad if he could keep the bird, and they said, "Yes."

So he hung the cage up in his room, and they've kept it a secret ever since.

Telling Stories

Sometimes we hear a story that is so good, we want to tell it to our friends. Folktales can be like that. So can fairy tales and legends.

Once Upon a Time . . .

This chapter will help you tell stories. First you will read a folktale. (You can use this story for practice.) Then you will learn about some great storytelling tips.

MODEL Story

The Three Billy Goats Gruff

Once upon a time, there were three billy goats named Gruff. They wanted to go up to the hillside to eat, but they had to cross a bridge to get there. Under this bridge, lived a great, ugly troll.

The youngest Billy Goat Gruff was the first to cross the bridge. *Trip, trap! Trip, trap! Trip, trap!*

"Who's that trip-trapping over my bridge?" yelled the troll.

"It is I, the youngest Billy Goat Gruff. I am going up to the hillside to eat," said the scared little billy goat.

"Well, I'm going to gobble you up!" said the troll.

"Don't eat *me*. I'm too little," said the billy goat. "Wait for the second Billy Goat Gruff. He's bigger."

"Very well," said the troll.

Then the second Billy Goat Gruff walked across the bridge. *Trip, trap! Trip, trap! Trip, trap!*

"Who's that trip-trapping over my bridge?" yelled the troll.

"It is I, the second Billy Goat Gruff. I am going up to the hillside to eat."

$\Rightarrow$

"Well, I'm going to gobble you up!" said the troll.

"Don't eat *me*. I'm not big enough," said the billy goat. "Wait for the oldest Billy Goat Gruff. He's much bigger."

"Very well," said the troll.

Just then the oldest Billy Goat Gruff walked across the bridge. *Trip, trap! Trip, trap! Trip, trap! Trip, trap!* He was very, very big.

"Who's that trip-trapping over my bridge?" yelled the troll.

"It is I, the oldest Billy Goat Gruff!" said the brave billy goat in a loud voice.

"Well, I'm going to gobble you up!" yelled the troll.

"Well, come along then! And I'll crush you to bits!" said the big Billy Goat Gruff.

Up rushed the troll, and the big Billy Goat Gruff took care of him in no time! After that, the oldest billy goat went up to the hillside with his brothers.

There the three billy goats got so fat, they were hardly able to walk home again.

So . . . snip, snap, snout, this tale's told out.

Storytelling TIPS

CHOOSE a story you really like—one that is not too long.

WRITE down the first and the last lines on different note cards. (Half sheets of paper work, too.) This way, you can read the beginning and the ending if you want to.

PRACTISE telling your story. Picture it in your head as you go along.

MAKE more note cards if you need them. Write down short clues to help you remember the main story parts.

USE your best voice. Add special feeling to important lines. (Don't talk too fast.)

TELL your story to your classmates or your family.

Giving Oral Reports

Do you have a collection? Do you know how to make something? Have you just read about an interesting subject?

Telling and Showing

You can share your special information in an oral report. An **oral report** is part telling and part showing. You tell important facts about your subject. And you show pictures or examples to go with the facts.

Planning Your Report

In the **beginning** . . .

- Name your subject in an interesting way.

In the **middle** . . .

- Give some main facts about your subject.
- Have pictures, charts, or examples to show.

In the **end** . . .

- Tell why this subject is important for you, or for others.

 To help you remember things, list your main ideas on note cards.

Giving Your Report

- **Use** your best outside voice. (Don't speak too fast!)
- **Look** at your classmates.
- **Try** to stand still.

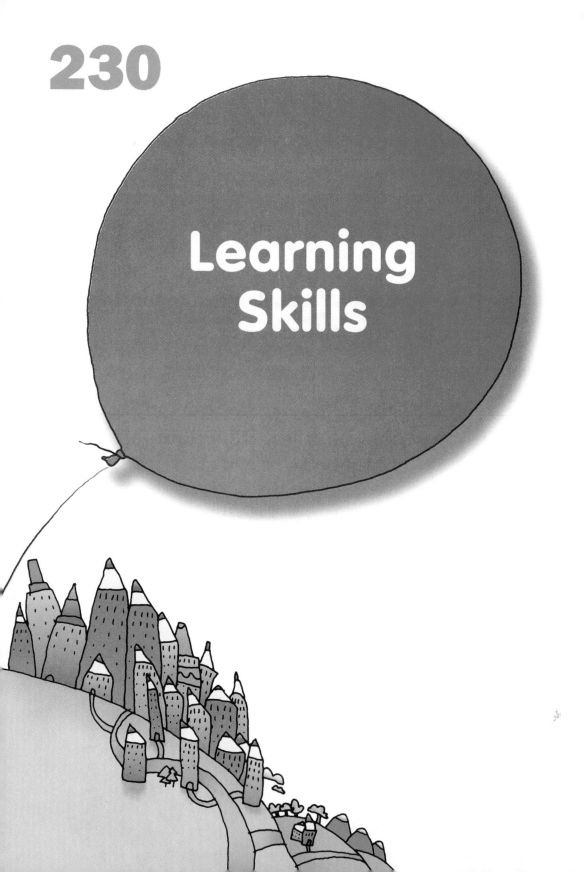

Learning Skills

Getting Organized

To play a board game, you have to get organized. You must get out all the pieces, and set them up in the right way.

Thinking on Paper

When you think about an important subject, you have to get organized, too. This chapter will show you how.

Clustering

A **cluster** helps you remember details about a subject. Write your subject in the middle of your paper. Circle it. Then write the details around your subject.

Uncle Phil brought cookies

a captain drove the boat

my best boat ride

Dad, Uncle Phil, and me

we saw seals

a pelican dove in the water

Clustering helps you remember details for all-about-me stories.

Describing a Subject

A **describing wheel** helps you describe a subject. Write your subject in the middle of the wheel. Write your describing words on the spokes.

Describing words can be things you see, hear, feel, smell, or taste.

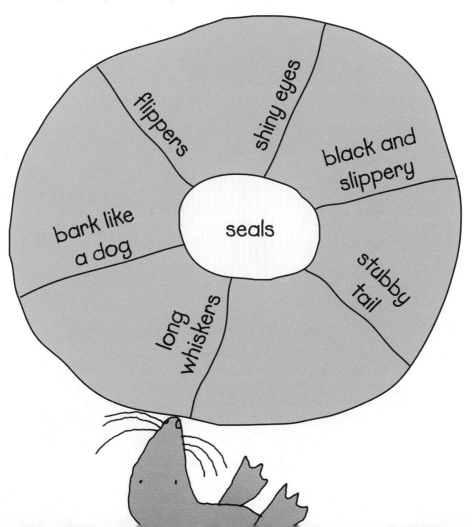

Comparing Two Subjects

A **Venn diagram** helps you compare two subjects. It has three spaces to fill in.

In spaces 1 and 2, you show how two subjects are different. In space 3, you show how the subjects are alike.

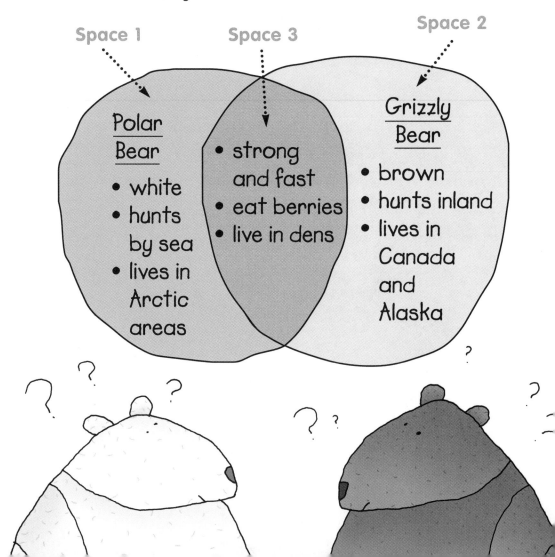

Space 1

Space 3

Space 2

Polar
Bear

- white
- hunts
  by sea
- lives in
  Arctic
  areas

- strong
  and fast
- eat berries
- live in dens

Grizzly
Bear

- brown
- hunts inland
- lives in
  Canada
  and
  Alaska

Making a Story Map

A **story map** helps you remember the important parts in a story. You can write words or draw pictures for the parts of a story.

Jack and the Beanstalk

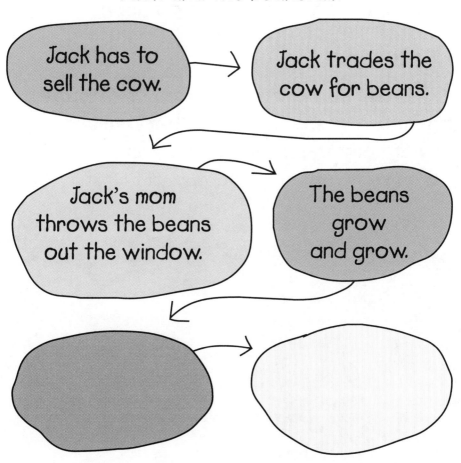

Working in Groups

Everybody works in groups. Doctors and firefighters work in groups. So do cookie bakers and second graders!

Teaming Up

Why do we work in groups? Groups help us finish big jobs. What must everybody in a group remember to do? Everybody must get along and try hard.

Planning TIPS

TALK about your assignment or job. Make sure everybody understands it.

SHARE your ideas. Take turns and listen carefully.

PLAN the work. Everybody should have a job to do.

PUT your plan on paper.

Group Plan

1. Our job is to _plan a welcome party_ .

2. Our due date is _Friday_ .

3. Things we need to do:

- Vijay and Tonya will bring cookies.
- Steve and Marcie will make a banner.
- Tonya will write a welcome speech.

Taking Tests

School keeps you busy. You read and write. You practise new skills. You make things. And you take tests!

Learning and Showing

Tests are not as much fun as some of the things you do. But they are important. This chapter will help you become a good test taker.

Matching Test

A **matching** test gives two lists of words. You must find the words from each list that go together.

- Study both lists very carefully.
- Then start with the first word in the left column. Try it with each word in the right column until you make a match.

Example:

MAKING COMPOUND WORDS

Directions: Draw a line between the words in both lists that go together.

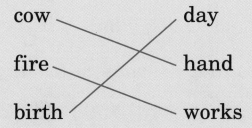

cow   day

fire   hand

birth   works

Multiple-Choice Test

A **multiple-choice** test gives a list of sentences to complete. You must pick the best choice to complete each sentence.

- Read the sentence with each choice.
- Then reread the sentence with your best choice. Be sure it makes sense.

Example:

FARM ANIMALS

Directions: Fill in the circle before the word that best completes each sentence.

1. A baby sheep is called a _____.

    (a) calf   **(b) lamb**   (c) fawn

2. A group of sheep is called a _____.

    (a) fawn   (b) band   **(c) flock**

Fill-in-the-Blank Test

A **fill-in-the-blank** test gives a list of sentences to complete. You must write the correct word or words in the blanks.

- Read each sentence very carefully.
- Count how many blanks you need to fill.
- Be sure your answer makes sense.

Example:

DAYS OF THE WEEK

Directions: Fill in the blanks to make each sentence complete.

1. ___Monday___ is the first weekday.

2. ___Saturday___ and ___Sunday___ are weekend days.

Short-Answer Test

A **short-answer** test gives you questions to answer in sentences.

- Read the question.
- Think about your answer.
- Write your sentence. Use a few words from the question in your sentence.

Example:

WEATHER

Directions: Answer each question in a complete sentence.

1. What are clouds made of?
   Clouds are made of tiny drops of water.

2. What is a blizzard?
   A blizzard is a snowstorm with strong winds.

Test-Taking TIPS

WRITE your name on your paper.

FOLLOW along as your teacher goes over the directions.

ASK questions if you do not understand something.

ANSWER the questions you know.

SKIP over the ones you're not sure of.

Then **GO BACK** to the unanswered questions.

Check to make sure you answered all the questions.

The Proofreader's GUIDE

The Proofreader's Guide

Using Punctuation

A "walk" signal tells us to go. A "don't walk" signal tells us to stop. These signals are very important.

Stopping and Going

Punctuation marks are signals we use in writing. For example, we use a period to signal a stop at the end of a sentence. You can learn about using punctuation in this chapter.

When to Use a Period

At the End of a Telling Sentence

George and Martha are silly.

After an Abbreviation

Mr. Plant

Ms. Blossom

Dr. Weed

Between Dollars and Cents

I have $2.25 in my pocket.

When to Use a Question Mark

After a Question

Who sat on my lunch?

When to Use an Exclamation Point

After an "Excited" Word

Wow! Awesome! Yuck!

After a Sentence Showing Strong Feelings

There's a skunk on the playground!

When to Use a Comma

**Between a City
and a Province**
   Hamilton, Ontario

**Between the Day
and the Year**
   July 1, 1867

After the Greeting in a Letter
   Dear Grandpa,

After the Closing in a Letter
   Love,
   Liz

Between Words in a Series
I love red, purple, and silver.

To Separate Interruptions
My big sister, however, can't come with us.

To Help Set Off a Speaker's Words
Ross said, "I love kickball!"

A comma looks like a period with a tail on it (,).

252

When to Use an Apostrophe

To Make a Contraction

Contraction	Short for
don't	do not
we'll	we will
hasn't	has not
can't	cannot

To Show That Someone Owns Something

my brother's frog
(One person owns the frog.)

the teachers' cars
(Two or more people own cars.)

When to Use Quotation Marks

Before and After a Speaker's Words

"I love carrots," said Chui.

For Titles of Stories and Poems

I called my story "Our New Pet."

When to Use Underlining

For Titles of Books and Magazines

I just read Kele's Secret.

Checking Mechanics

Rules help us in many ways. We have rules that help us keep safe. We have rules that help us play games. We also have rules that help us with our writing.

Rules for Writing

This chapter lists rules for the **mechanics of writing**. (*Say* mə kan′ iks.) You will learn about using capital letters, writing plurals, and much more. *Remember:* Rules help us write!

Using Capital Letters

For the First Word in a Sentence
➚ Fireflies light up the garden.

For a Speaker's First Word
Mr. Smith said, "Look at this spiderweb." ➚

For Names and Titles
➜ Jackie Wilson
➜ Dr. Small

For the Word "I"
What will I say to him?
➚

Using
Capital Letters

For Titles of Books, Stories, Poems, . . .

→ Franklin's Blanket   (book)

"Lost in the Woods"   (story)

"Elephant for Sale"   (poem)

Chickadee   (magazine)

For Days, Months, and Holidays

→ Friday   January   Thanksgiving

For Names of Places

→ Canada   Rocky Mountains

Alberta   Main Street

North Bay   CN Tower

Making Plurals

Add "s" to make the plural of most nouns.

    bug – bug**s**   wing – wing**s**

Add "es" to make the plural of nouns ending in *s, x, sh,* and *ch.*

    glass – glass**es**   bush – bush**es**

Change the word to make the plural of some nouns.

    child – **children**   man – **men**

Change the "y" to "i" and add "es" to nouns with a consonant before the *y.*

    sky – sk**ies**   story – stor**ies**

Using Abbreviations

For Titles of People
➔ Mr.   Ms.   Mrs.   Dr.

For Addresses on Envelopes

MS JOAN CAPEWELL
FIRST CANADIAN BANK
101 MAIN ST
SUDBURY, ON P3C 3E6

(Remember to print neatly.)

Post Office Address Abbreviations

Avenue	AVE	North	N
Boulevard	BLVD	Road	RD
Court	CRT	Rural Route	RR
Crescent	CRES	South	S
Drive	DR	Square	SQ
East	E	Street	ST
Highway	HWY	West	W

Post Office Provincial Abbreviations

Alberta	**AB**
British Columbia	**BC**
Manitoba	**MB**
New Brunswick	**NB**
Newfoundland and Labrador	**NF**
Northwest Territories	**NT**
Nova Scotia	**NS**
Nunavut Territory	**NT**
Ontario	**ON**
Prince Edward Island	**PE**
Quebec	**QC**
Saskatchewan	**SK**
Yukon Territory	**YT**

Checking Your Spelling

This spelling list includes many of the important words you will use in your writing. Check this list when you are not sure how to spell a word. (Also check a classroom dictionary for help.)

A

about
again
alone
animal
ant
are
ask
aunt
away

B

back
bad
bank
bed
been
before
believe
bell
best
big
black
blocks
blue
boat
bones
book
born
box
bricks
bright
broke

broom
brother
brown
burn
but
by

C

cake
call
candle
candy
cards
chicken
chicks
children
clean
clock
colours
comes
cookies
corner

could
crowded

D

daddy
dance
dark
desks
didn't
doesn't
dog
doll
dollars
done
don't
door
dream
drop
dropping
duck

E

each
eat
eggs
eight
eye

F

fall
farm
fast
feather
feel
fight
fire
five
floor
flowers
fly
flying

food
foot
for
forgot
fort
four
Friday
frog
front
full
fun
funny

G

game
give
going
good
grass
green

H

hair
half
hall
hand
happen
hard
has
head
help
hid
hidden
high
hill
hit
hook
hope
horse
hot
hours
how
hurt

I

I
ice
I'm
its
it's
I've

J

jam
jelly
just

K

keep
kids
kite
kitten
knew

L

lady
land
last
laugh
let
letter
licked
light
log
lonely
look
lot
loud
love

M

make
many
may
men

milk
Monday
money
monkey
month
moon
more
morning
most
mouse
move

N

name
need
new
next
nice
night
nine
not
now

O

okay
once
one
open
orange
other
ours

P

party
penny
play
please
poor
porch
post
pour
pretty
pull
purple

Q

quick
quiet

R

rabbit
rain
ready
really
ride
road
rode
room
rope

S

said
Saturday
says
school

seven
shoes
should
six
skies
sleep
socks
soft
something
soon
sound
stairs
stick
still
stopping
store
storm
street
summer
Sunday
sure
swimming
swing

T

take
teacher
teeth
tell
ten
thank
their
there
they're
three
Thursday
told
tooth
train
tree
trucks
try
Tuesday
turkeys
turn
two

U

under
until
use

V

van
very

W

wall
water
weather
Wednesday
week
went
what
when
where
white

who
why
wish
women
won
wool
work
would

X

X-ray

Y

year
yellow
your
you're

Z

zoo

Spelling TIPS

Make a SPELLING NOTEBOOK

Save one or two pages for each letter in the alphabet. Write **A** at the top of the "**A word**" pages, **B** at the top of the "**B word**" pages, and so on. When you find words that are hard, add them to your notebook.

Read over your notebook often. You will soon know how to spell the words.

Use a SPELLING PLAN

Use a plan to practise a new word:

* Look at the word and say it.
* Spell it aloud.
* Cover the word and spell it on paper.
* Check the spelling.
* If you made a mistake, try again.

Learn Some
SPELLING TRICKS

For some words, you may make the same mistake over and over again. When this happens, try one of these tricks:

* Say the word aloud. Say the hard letters the loudest.

    Say rabbit like **rabBIT**.

* Spell the word on paper. Underline the hard letters, or print them bigger than the other letters.

* Think of a saying to help you remember a spelling:

    A bear is hidDEN in the DEN.

Using the Right Word

Some words sound alike, but they have different spellings. They also have different meanings. These words are called **homophones**.

ant   An **ant** crawled onto my finger.

aunt   My **aunt** likes to tell jokes.

ate   Liz **ate** lunch with me.

eight   I have **eight** crayons.

bare   My bare hands are freezing.

bear   Ira has a teddy bear.

blew   Dakota blew the biggest bubble.

blue   A robin's egg is blue.

dear   My grandma is a dear woman.

deer   The deer ran into the woods.

eye   Lu winks her eye.

I   I love to draw cats.

for   Ms. Nelson made cookies for us.

four   Nick ate four tacos.

hear   I like to hear birds sing.

here   Who sits here?

knew   I knew my ABC's last year.

new   We have a new girl in our class.

know   Do you know her name?

no   Robert said, "No, I don't."

made   We made popcorn for a snack.

maid   Amelia Bedelia is a funny maid.

meat   Some people don't eat meat.

meet   I'll meet you at the clubhouse.

one	My baby brother is one year old.
won	Liz won a prize at the fair.
read	Mr. Lee read a funny poem.
red	I gave him a red apple.
road	Tony lives on a country road.
rode	He rode his bike to school.
sea	A sea is a big body of water.
see	Come and see my pet snake.

Visitors
Welcome

sew   My grandma likes to sew for me.

so   I'll hurry so we're not late.

son   My dad is the son of his dad.

sun   Plants need sun and water.

tail   A beaver has a flat tail.

tale   Cinderella is a fairy tale.

their   We used their bikes.
            (*Their* shows ownership.)

there   There are four of them.

they're They're mountain bikes.
            (*they're* = they are)

to	I like to read funny books.
two	I read two joke books today.
too	Joe likes joke books, too.

wear	I like to wear floppy hats.
where	Where are you going?

wood	The fence is made of wood.
would	Dawn would like to go home.

your	What is your favourite video?
you're	You're a great singer.
	(*you're* = you are)

Checking Your Sentences

What do I need to know?

A **sentence** tells a complete idea and has two parts.

1. The subject is the naming part.
2. The verb tells what the subject is doing.

My <u>mom</u> <u>drives</u> a motorbike.
  subject verb

A **sentence** begins with a capital letter. It ends with a period, a question mark, or an exclamation point.

→ Grandpa climbs trees. ←

Kinds of Sentences

A **telling sentence** (*declarative*) makes a statement.

Soccer is my favourite game.

An **asking sentence** (*interrogative*) asks a question.

Will you play with me?

A **directing sentence** (*imperative*) gives directions or a command.

Kick with the side of your foot.

An **exclamatory sentence** shows strong feelings.

Watch out for the ball!

Understanding Our Language

All of the words we use fit into eight groups. These groups are called the **parts of speech**.

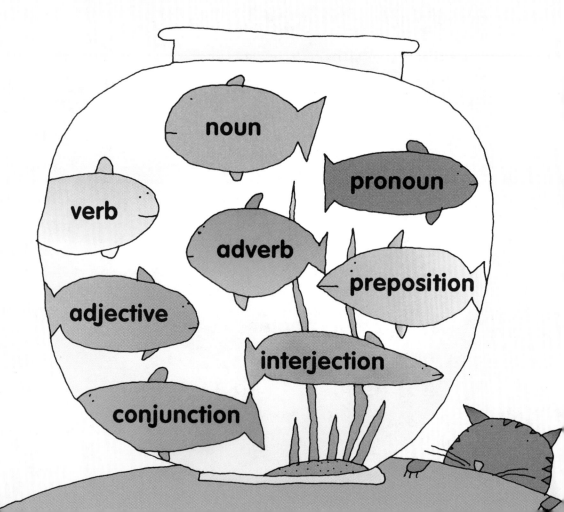

What is a noun?

A **noun** names a person, place, or thing.
girl   house   bike

Nouns can be **singular** or **plural**.
singular: neighbour   house
plural: neighbours houses

Nouns can be **common** or **proper**.
common: boy   street
proper: Gus   Oak Street

A **possessive noun** shows ownership.
Julie's flute
the **boys'** tubas

What is a pronoun?

A **pronoun** is a word that takes the place of a noun. Here are some pronouns.

I	me	my	he
him	his	she	her
you	your	it	its
we	us	our	they
them	their		

How are pronouns used?

Pronouns stand for nouns in sentences.

Holly played a game.

She hid the penny.

(*She* is a pronoun.)

Erik made cookies.

Then **he** ate **them**.

(*He* and *them* are pronouns.)

What is a verb?

A **verb** shows action or helps complete a thought or an idea.
   Spot **barks** at my neighbour.
   Mr. Wilson **is** so mad!

Some verbs tell what is happening now, or in the **present**.
   George **slips** on the banana peel.

Some verbs tell what happened in the **past**.
   Sarah **walked** her dog.

Some verbs tell what will happen in the **future**.
   I **will find** some shells.

What are the different forms of verbs?

Many verbs are **regular**.
You can add *ed* to them.

> I **laugh**.
> I **laughed**.
> I **have laughed**.
>> (with helping word)

Some verbs are **irregular**. You usually can't add *ed* to them. They change in different ways.

> I **eat**.
> I **ate**.
> I **have eaten**.
>> (with helping word)

 TIP There is a list of irregular verbs on the next page.

Common Irregular Verbs

Present	Past	With Helping Word
am, is, are	was, were	been
begin	began	begun
break	broke	broken
catch	caught	caught
come	came	come
do	did	done
draw	drew	drawn
eat	ate	eaten
fall	fell	fallen
give	gave	given
go	went	gone
hide	hid	hidden, hid
know	knew	known
ride	rode	ridden
ring	rang	rung
run	ran	run
see	saw	seen
sing	sang, sung	sung
take	took	taken
throw	threw	thrown
write	wrote	written

What is an adjective?

An **adjective** describes a noun or pronoun.

> **Many** animals live in the jungle.
> An anaconda is a **giant** snake!

An **adjective** sometimes compares *two* nouns (or pronouns).

> An ant is **smaller** than an anaconda.

An adjective sometimes compares *more than two* nouns.

> An anteater is the **oddest** animal.

The words *a, an,* and *the* are **articles**.
Use *a* before a consonant sound:

> **a** parrot

Use *an* before a vowel sound:

> **an** otter

What are the other parts of speech?

An **adverb** is a word that describes a verb.

Erin ran **quickly**.   She fell **down**.

A **preposition** is used to help make a statement.

Maya laughed **at** the joke.

Joe sat **on** the beach.

A **conjunction** connects words or ideas.

I will dance **or** sing.

First I cried **and** then I laughed.

An **interjection** shows excitement.

Wow! Did you see that bug?

Yuck! I hate creepy crawlers!

Using Theme Words

DAYS/MONTHS

Sunday   Monday

Tuesday   Wednesday

Thursday   Friday   Saturday

January   February

March   April   May

June   July   August

September   October

November   December

SEASON/WEATHER WORDS

winter   spring   summer   fall

sun   sunny   wind   windy

breeze   breezy   degrees

rain   snow   sleet   fog

cold   hot   lightning

storm   tornado

hurricane   clouds

thermometer

thunder   warm

temperature   hail

FOOD WORDS

apples   oranges   bananas

grapes   lettuce   peaches

strawberries   broccoli   potatoes

corn   carrots   bread   beans

peanut butter   spaghetti

jam   pizza   cookies

cupcakes   milk   yogurt

ice cream   hamburgers   rice

hot dogs   chicken   cereal

sandwiches   muffins

COMMUNITY WORDS

apartment   town   city

house   police officer   doctor

mail carrier   shopping mall

drugstore   post office   church

neighbour   store   firefighter

street   movie theatre   school

plumber   teacher   grocery store

hospital   librarian   nurse

neighbourhood   gas station

garbage collector

The Student ALMANAC

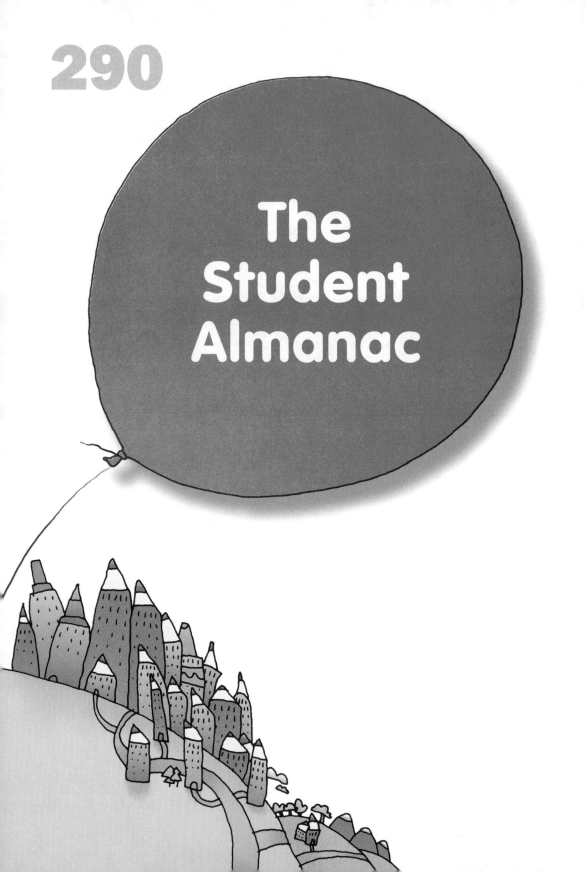

The Student Almanac

Useful Tables and Lists

The tables and lists in this section are interesting and fun to use.

Sign Language

Braille Alphabet and Braille Numbers

a	b	c	d	e	f	g	h	i	j
1	2	3	4	5	6	7	8	9	0

k	l	m	n	o	p	q	r	s	t

u	v	w	x	y	z	Capital Sign	Numeral Sign

Roman Numerals

1	I	6	VI	11	XI
2	II	7	VII	12	XII
3	III	8	VIII	50	L
4	IV	9	IX	100	C
5	V	10	X	1000	M

Saying Hello and Goodbye

This table will help you say "hello" and "goodbye" in different languages.

Language	Hello or Good Day	Goodbye
Chinese (Mandarin dialect)	dzău	dzàijyàn
Farsi (Iran)	salaam سلام	khoda hafez خدا حافظ
French	bonjour	au revoir
German	Guten Tag	Auf Wiedersehen
Hebrew	shalom	shalom
Spanish	hola	adiós
Swahili	neno la kusalimu rafiki au mtani	kwa heri

Animal Facts

Animal	Male	Female	Young	Group
Bear	He-bear	She-bear	Cub	Sleuth
Cat	Tom	Queen	Kitten	Clutter/Clowder
Cattle	Bull	Cow	Calf	Drove/Herd
Chicken	Rooster	Hen	Chick	Brood/Flock
Deer	Buck	Doe	Fawn	Herd
Dog	Dog	Bitch	Pup	Pack/Kennel
Donkey	Jack	Jenny	Foal	Herd/Pace
Duck	Drake	Duck	Duckling	Brace/Herd
Elephant	Bull	Cow	Calf	Herd
Fox	Dog	Vixen	Cub/Kit	Skulk
Goat	Billy	Nanny	Kid	Tribe/Herd
Goose	Gander	Goose	Gosling	Flock/Gaggle
Horse	Stallion	Mare	Filly/Colt	Herd
Lion	Lion	Lioness	Cub	Pride
Monkey	Male	Female	Boy/Girl	Band/Troop
Rabbit	Buck	Doe	Bunny	Nest/Warren
Sheep	Ram	Ewe	Lamb	Flock/Drove
Swine	Boar	Sow	Piglet	Litter/Herd
Whale	Bull	Cow	Calf	Gam/Pod/Herd

Animal Speeds

These speeds are for short distances. For example, a human could not run 45 km in one hour. However, for a short time, someone could reach that speed.

KM PER HOUR	1	16	32	48	64	80	96	112	128
Osprey (flies)									128
Cheetah								112	
Quarter Horse						75			
Coyote					69				
Ostrich (runs)					64				
Greyhound					62				
Giraffe				51					
White-tailed Deer				48					
Grizzly Bear				48					
Cat				48					
Human				45					
Elephant				40					
Snake			32						
Giant Tortoise	0.27								
Snail	0.05								

Measurements

Metric System

Here are some common metric measures.

Length (how far)

1 millimetre (mm) . ⟵······ millimetre

1 centimetre (cm) = **10 millimetres** ⟵······ 10 millimetres

1 metre (m) = **100 centimetres** = **1000 millimetres**

1 kilometre (km) = **1000 metres** =
  100 000 centimetres = **1 000 000 millimetres**

Mass (how heavy)

1 gram (g)

1 kilogram (kg) = **1000 grams**

Capacity (how much something can hold)

1 millilitre (mL)

1 litre (L) = **1000 millilitres**

Some Measurement Facts

The African elephant can grow to have a mass between 5400 and 7200 kg. Its tusks can measure more than 3 m long and have a mass as much as 90 kg each. The elephant's amazing trunk can be over 2 m long and hold almost 5 L of water.

The air in a sneeze can travel over 160 km/h.

The Atlantic giant squid has eyeballs as much as 40 cm wide. Squids can measure over 15 m long.

On a clear day, the peregrine falcon can spot a pigeon almost 8 km away.

Our Sun is actually a star. It has a temperature of 15 400 000°C—that's more than five hundred thousand times hotter than a hot summer day of 30°C here on Earth!

Hair grows almost 2 mm a week, or just over 9 cm a year.

The human body has almost 96 000 km of blood vessels.

Our Solar System

The nine planets in our solar system orbit around the sun.

Mercury has the shortest year. It is 88 days long.

Venus spins the slowest. It takes 243 days to spin around once.

Earth supports life for plants, animals, and people.

Mars has less gravity than Earth. A 23 kg person would weigh about 9 kg on Mars.

Jupiter is the largest planet. It is more than 10 times bigger than Earth.

Saturn has at least seven rings. It also has the most moons—23.

Uranus has the most rings—15.

Neptune is the coldest planet.

Pluto is the smallest planet.

Sun

Mercury   Venus

Earth   Mars

Jupiter

Saturn

Uranus

Neptune

Pluto

All About Maps

Maps help you in many ways. For example, a school map helps you find your way in a new school. A weather map can tell you if you need to wear a coat today.

Around the World

The maps in this chapter help you learn about places in the world and in our country. You will also learn how to read maps, plus much more.

Directions

Sometimes a map shows the direction "north."

If a map doesn't show this, north is probably at the top of the page, and south is at the bottom. East is to the right of the page, and west is to the left.

Map Legend and Symbols

The **legend** is a list that explains the symbols used

CANADA

⊗ **National Capital**

★ **Provincial/Territorial Capitals**

----- **Provincial/Territorial Boundary**

on a map. Symbols are like little signs that tell what is on a map. Here is the legend for the map on page 305 in your handbook.

Three **symbols** are listed in this legend. There is a symbol for the national capital (⊗), for the provincial/territorial capitals (★), and for the provincial/territorial boundaries (-----).

The Globe

The best map of the world is a globe. A **globe** shows our earth as it really is: round!

Equator ....

Prime Meridian ....

Lines of Latitude and Longitude

Lines of **latitude** go around the globe. The **equator** is the most famous line of latitude. It goes around the middle of the globe.

Lines of **longitude** go up and down, from the North Pole to the South Pole. The **prime meridian** is the most famous line of longitude. It passes through Greenwich, England.

THE WORLD
Continents and Oceans

ARCTIC OCEAN

PACIFIC OCEAN

ASIA

AUSTRALIA

INDIAN OCEAN

EUROPE

AFRICA

EQUATOR

ATLANTIC OCEAN

ARCTIC OCEAN

NORTH AMERICA

SOUTH AMERICA

PACIFIC OCEAN

N

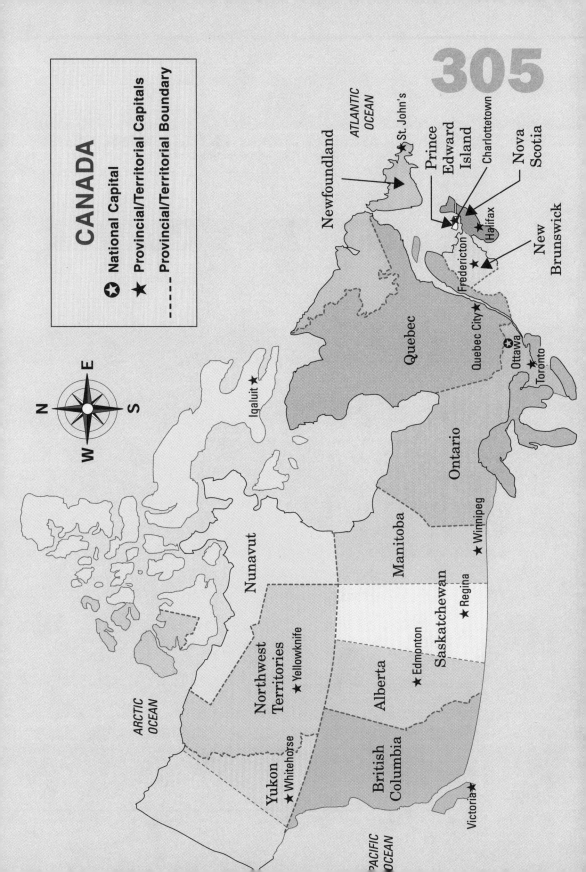

CANADA

- ✪ National Capital
- ★ Provincial/Territorial Capitals
- ----- Provincial/Territorial Boundary

ATLANTIC OCEAN

Newfoundland

★ St. John's

Prince Edward Island

Charlottetown

Nova Scotia

Halifax

New Brunswick

Fredericton ★

Quebec

Quebec City ★

✪ Ottawa

Toronto ★

Ontario

Winnipeg ★

Manitoba

Igaluit ★

Nunavut

Saskatchewan

Regina ★

Northwest Territories

Yellowknife ★

Alberta

Edmonton ★

Yukon

Whitehorse ★

British Columbia

Victoria ★

ARCTIC OCEAN

PACIFIC OCEAN

N E S W

Provinces, Territories, and their Capitals

Province/Territory	Capital
Alberta	Edmonton
British Columbia	Victoria
Manitoba	Winnipeg
New Brunswick	Fredericton
Newfoundland	St. John's
Northwest Territories	Yellowknife
Nova Scotia	Halifax
Nunavut Territory	Iqaluit
Ontario	Toronto
Prince Edward Island	Charlottetown
Quebec	Quebec City
Saskatchewan	Regina
Yukon Territory	Whitehorse

Facts About Canada

POPULATION
27 297 000

TOTAL AREA
9 970 610 km^2

LARGEST CITY (POPULATION)
Toronto, ON   3 893 046

LONGEST RIVER
Mackenzie, BC   4241 km

LARGEST LAKE
Superior, ON   82 100 km^2

HIGHEST WATERFALL
Della Falls, BC   440 m

LARGEST ISLAND
Baffin, NT   507 451 km^2

HIGHEST POINT
Mt. Logan, YT   5959 m

Working with Math

You use math a lot. You add and subtract numbers, you count money, and you tell time. You also measure things, and so on.

From Adding to Telling Time

This chapter will help you become "math smart." The first part shows you how to solve word problems. The second part gives helpful math tables and charts.

Word Problems

Word problems are like little stories. (Some teachers call them story problems.) But they do not have endings. You make the endings by solving the problems!

Example Word Problem

Suzanne has 2 bags of cookies. Each bag has 3 cookies inside. Suzanne's brother gives her another bag with 3 cookies inside. How many cookies does Suzanne have in all?

Fun Learning

Word problems like this one are fun to solve—if you know how to do it! We will show you how on the next two pages.

310

Solving Word Problems

1 **Read the problem carefully.**
Look for important words such as "how many" and "in all."

> **How many cookies does Suzanne have in all?**

- If you don't understand part of the problem, ask for help.

2 **Decide what to do.**

- Do you have to add or subtract some numbers?

- Or do you have to do two things—maybe add and then subtract?

3

Do the problem. Decide how you will solve the problem. You could draw pictures, use counters, or write a math problem.

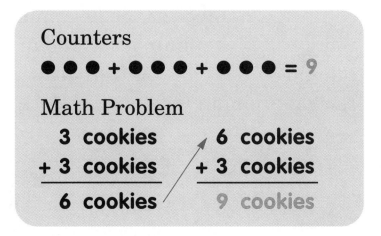

Counters

● ● ● + ● ● ● + ● ● ● = 9

Math Problem

3 cookies	6 cookies
+ 3 cookies	+ 3 cookies
6 cookies	9 cookies

4

Check your answer. Start with your answer and work backward.

9 cookies	6 cookies
- 3 cookies	- 3 cookies
6 cookies	3 cookies

● Or solve the problem a different way. You should get the same answer.

Math Tables and Charts

Addition Facts

Pick a number at the beginning of a row (4). Pick a number at the top of a column (7). Find your answer where the row and column meet (4) + (7) = (11).

+	1	2	3	4	5	6	7	8	9	10
1	2	3	4	5	6	7	8	9	10	11
2	3	4	5	6	7	8	9	10	11	12
3	4	5	6	7	8	9	10	11	12	13
4	5	6	7	8	9	10	11	12	13	14
5	6	7	8	9	10	11	12	13	14	15
6	7	8	9	10	11	12	13	14	15	16
7	8	9	10	11	12	13	14	15	16	17
8	9	10	11	12	13	14	15	16	17	18
9	10	11	12	13	14	15	16	17	18	19
10	11	12	13	14	15	16	17	18	19	20

Skip Counting

2's	2	4	6	8	10	12	14	16
3's	3	6	9	12	15	18	21	24
4's	4	8	12	16	20	24	28	32
5's	5	10	15	20	25	30	35	40

Place Value Chart

Here are the place values for 3752:

3	**7**	**5**	**2**
thousands	hundreds	tens	ones

3 in the thousands' place is **3000**
7 in the hundreds' place is **700**
5 in the tens' place is **50**
2 in the ones' place is **2**

You read this four-digit number as **three thousand seven hundred fifty-two**.

Fractions

A **fraction** is a part of something. A fraction has a top number and a bottom number, like this example:

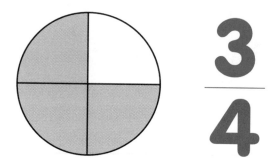

Reading Fractions

The bottom number (4) tells you the circle is divided into four equal parts. The top number (3) tells you that three of the parts are being named. You read 3/4 as **three-quarters**.

More Examples

$\frac{1}{2}$ one-half

$\frac{5}{6}$ five-sixths

Counting Money

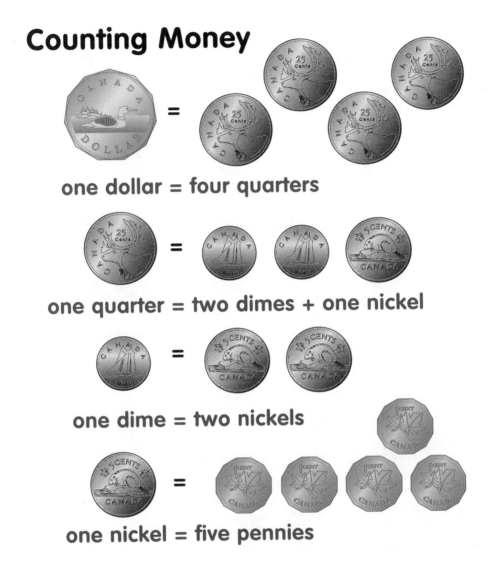

one dollar = four quarters

one quarter = two dimes + one nickel

one dime = two nickels

one nickel = five pennies

How much money?

If you counted all the money shown above, you would have two dollars and eighty cents. You would write $2.80.

Telling Time

hour hand ⋯⋯⋯

minute hand ⋯⋯⋯

**one hour = 60 minutes
one-half hour = 30 minutes**

2:00

When the minute hand (long hand) is on 12, you write 00 for the minutes.

3:25

When the
minute hand
is on a number,
count by 5's
from the top to
tell the time.
(5, 10, 15,
20, **25**)

3:26

When the
minute hand is
between numbers,
count by 5's from the
top. Then add the minute marks past the
last number to find the time. (25 + 1 = **26**)

Improving Handwriting

Do you use manuscript or cursive letters? You will find charts for both types of letters in this chapter. The checklist and tips on the last page will help you write neatly.

manuscript

My name is Al.

cursive

My name is Al.

Manuscript Letters

A B C D E
F G H I J K
L M N O P
Q R S T U
V W X Y Z

a b c d e f g
h i j k l m n
o p q r s t
u v w x y z

Cursive Letters

A B C D E

F G H I J K

L M N O P

Q R S T U

V W X Y Z

a b c d e f

g h i j k l

m n o p q

r s t u v

w x y z

Handwriting TIPS

SIT up straight when you write.

HOLD your pencil comfortably, not too tightly.

USE your best handwriting for final copies.

Handwriting Checklist

✔ Are my letters formed correctly?

✔ Do all my letters slant the same way?

✔ Do I have enough space between words?

✔ Do I like how my writing looks?

TIPS for Writers

1. Read, read, read.

2. Pick good ideas.

3. Try different forms of writing.

4. Practise, practise, practise.

5. Share your writing.

6. Have fun.

Proofreading Checklist

✔ Did you capitalize the first word in each sentence?

✔ Did you capitalize names?

✔ Did you put a period, a question mark, or an exclamation point after each sentence?

✔ Did you spell your words correctly?

Index

The **index** helps you find information in your handbook. Let's say you want to learn how to write a poem. You can look in your index under "poetry" for help.